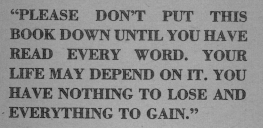

"PLEASE DON'T PUT THIS BOOK DOWN UNTIL YOU HAVE READ EVERY WORD. YOUR LIFE MAY DEPEND ON IT. YOU HAVE NOTHING TO LOSE AND EVERYTHING TO GAIN."

"I know I have seen the appearance of the finger of God against this nation. . . . My directions are simply to cry aloud and share these warnings in every way possible. . . . I know people will call me an alarmist, a sensationalist, and a preacher of doom and despair. Even well-meaning ministers and church leaders will refute the message as 'not from God'—before they have shut themselves in the secret closet of prayer to see if these things really be true. . . .

—DAVID WILKERSON

RACING TOWARD JUDGMENT

David Wilkerson

SPIRE BOOKS

FLEMING H. REVELL COMPANY
Old Tappan, New Jersey

RACING TOWARD JUDGMENT

A SPIRE BOOK

Published by Jove Publications, Inc.
for Fleming H. Revell Company

Spire Edition published November 1976
Fifth printing January 1979

Copyright © 1976 by David Wilkerson Youth Crusades

All Rights Reserved

Library of Congress Catalog Card Number: 76-22933

ISBN 0-8007-8276-3

Printed in the United States of America

SPIRE BOOKS are published by
Fleming H. Revell Company
Old Tappan, New Jersey 07675, U.S.A.

Contents

Introduction

I really don't care what people think about this book, pro or con. All I know is that God holds me responsible to proclaim the message He gives me.

I hear the sound of a trumpet. It is God's awesome warning that our nation is racing toward judgment. Let all the prophets of the positive talk up a boom. Let ministers and politicians peddle their optimistic gospel. As for me, I see black days of holy retribution and judgment just ahead. With an inner peace and joy that only God can give, I deliver this message with no apologies. This is a "doomsday" book! We Americans like to shut out all bad news. We rebel against ugly words like doom, gloom, recession, depression, judgment. But that doesn't change a thing. Like it or not, America is racing toward judgment.

There is absolutely nothing new about warning of coming earthquakes, drought, and financial chaos. Scientists on the West Coast are screaming out their warnings of major quakes they believe are coming very soon. Drought conditions already exist. Hundreds of farmers are even now headed for bankruptcy. New York and at least fifteen other major cities in America are on the brink of bankruptcy. Labor unrest, racial hatred, and runaway inflation are all time bombs that can abort recovery at any moment. We may have already reached the point in this country (crosscurrents of society are flowing so fast) that recovery is now beyond the reach of human ingenuity.

I am not a prophet, and I refuse to allow anyone to put that tag on me. But I am a watchman. Just one of many in this nation who now warn Americans to get ready for persecution and judgment. I have no sense of destiny, and I am not motivated by dreams or impressions. I have spent months studying my Bible, learning how God deals with societies and nations that forget Him. It was that long look back into historical prophecy that prompted my look into the future. God's methods of judgment may change with each generation, but His justice never changes. Now I don't have to say, "This, I prophesy." I can, with confidence, say, "This is what God will do, based on the record of His Word."

A few years ago I wrote a book entitled "The Vision." In it, I warned about many of the calamities that are befalling this nation and the world even now. The book created controversy among Christians everywhere. Many read only the first half of the book and threw it down. They were scared, angered, or unbelieving. If they had taken the time to read the rest of the book, they would have understood the real message I was preaching—namely, that God has everything under control. And that Christians have nothing to fear.

It is even more important for true believers to read all of this book. If you read only about the judgment and terror of the Lord and get turned off, you will miss the message completely. I want Christians to be able to lay this book down, after absorbing its full contents, and breathe this prayer: "Live or die, we are the Lord's." I want Christians to prepare for the future with joy, confidence, and hope.

I want those who are not ready to meet God to read this book with a reverential fear. And I pray that fear will lead to repentance and restoration.

Judgment is coming on America. Get ready.

1

The Party's Over

1. Judgment Is Coming

Please don't put this book down until you have read every word. Your life may depend on it. You have nothing to lose and everything to gain. Read carefully the following prophecy:

Unbelievable disasters are roaring down upon us like a whirlwind from the outer limits of the universe. Awesome calamities will soon fall on this nation and mankind will be terrified. This nation will stagger like a drunkard. Days of crushing confusion and terror will cause men's hearts to fail them for fear. Many parts of this country will languish, crops will wither, crime will become nearly uncontrollable, laws will be twisted and defied, and the economy will totter on the brink of total collapse.

The upraised fist of God is poised, ready to destroy pride and to condemn the self-acclaimed greatness of our nation. The peoples of this land are going to suffer for their blatant sins. The Commander of the armies of Heaven will soon come forth to shake this nation like a tent in a storm. The world will witness the curse of God against those who have twisted and forsaken His everlasting commandments. The joys and pleasures of life will soon be turned into mourning. The merrymakers will weep and sigh. Singing, happy days will give way to a time of mob rule, chaos in city streets, homes and shops locked up tight to keep out looters, and life will fall to its lowest ebb.

Priests and people, masters and slaves, buyers and sellers, lenders and borrowers, bankers and debtors—none will be spared. The land will be looted and its spirit crushed. Prophets of peace will go up and down the land deluding victims with foolish counsel that all is well.

Now then, I am sure your first reaction to the above prophecy may turn you off. You may be thinking to yourself, "It's just another doomsday sermon! Another prophet of calamity trying to scare people!" The truth of the matter is that history repeats itself. The predictions of coming calamities are not mine at all—they are the warnings of the prophet Isaiah directed at his society, centuries ago.

This fearless prophet saw a frightening vision of approaching calamities and cried out:

. . . God is telling me what He is going to do. I see the land plundered and destroyed. When I hear what God is going to do, my stomach constricts with burning pain; sharp pangs of horror come upon me . . . my mind reels: my heart races; I am gripped by an awful fear. I can no longer sleep and I lie awake, trembling.

(Isaiah 21:2–4)

Few would listen to this prophet of despair— especially the religious leaders, even though signs everywhere confirmed his vision. World armies were poised for attack. Leaders of various nations were preparing to betray one another to preserve national interests. Death echoed from the mountain tops. Valleys were filling up with anxious armies of hard-driving chariots. Archers crowded each other to practice their skills. Armories were being overtaken by government officials. So convinced the night of calamity was near, Isaiah called out one final message to the masses: "How much time is left? None! Your judgment day is dawning now. Turn quickly to God; seek Him now, or never. The party is over!" (Isaiah 21:11–12).

The party—over? Not as far as the masses were concerned. If calamity was truly coming, they would go for one more last fling. Listen to the heart cry of Prophet Isaiah, because it has everything to do with us today:

> Look! They are preparing a great banquet! They load the tables with food; they pull up their chairs. . . .
>
> (Isaiah 21:5 LB)

> Instead of weeping and preparing and repenting, they sing and dance and play. They feast and drink. They say to one another, "Eat, drink, and be merry, for tomorrow we may die."
>
> (Isaiah 22:12,13)

2. A Boom Before the Bust

This prophet lived in times of great prosperity. Babylon was a thriving, exciting city at the very zenith of growth and prosperity. Judah was an economically booming nation with its people safe and secure in their beautiful little homes. Jerusalem was a beautiful, peaceful city where people were busily engaged in buying, selling, marrying, divorcing, and indulging their every lust. Tyre was a booming seaport full of oceangoing vessels bringing merchandise from all over the world. It was the New York City of Isaiah's time, the merchandise mart of the world. It was an empire builder, a top trader of the world, a joyous land of tremendous history and tradition, sending out colonists to develop other nations. Life was one big party, and there seemed to be no

11

end to the good times. People had become totally conscious of security and pleasure.

But suddenly a man of God appears and a booming voice is heard throughout the land—"The party is over!" Where did this prophet of God get the audacity to walk from city to city in his bare feet crying,

> Bodies lying everywhere! That's what I see coming! Multitudes will be slain by plagues. Your leaders will flee and enemy armies will come crushing over the breaches in your collapsing walls. God will remove His protecting care, and all your feverish plans are in vain—the party is over—and that is final!
>
> (Isaiah 22:2,3,5,8–11, 14)

This prophet had seen a vision and it frightened him. He saw enemy armies roaring out of the Negev Desert to plunder and destroy that great city Babylon. He saw the bustling harbors of Tyre going up in smoke and predicted that city would come crashing down in such chaos it would go into a seventy-year depression. He saw Jerusalem and Judah being raped by enemy armies and the once proud inhabitants being paraded naked through foreign city streets. He warned them their homes would be looted and burned, their wives and children murdered, and that only a remnant would survive.

3. Few Will Believe

But who could believe such nonsense? This prophet of God was called a fanatic and was so maligned and ridiculed he began to question himself. He said to God, "They laugh at me and say I speak in parables; but I know that all you've told me is true." Babylon was destroyed by Elamites and Medes who came swarming in from the desert; Judah and Jerusalem were carried

12

away by enemy armies; and the seaport city of Tyre was gripped by a massive depression that brought it to ruin. It is all documented history. God did exactly what He said He would do, right on schedule.

> Tell them everything that I will do to them, but don't expect them to listen. Cry out your warnings, but don't expect them to respond. Say to them: This is the nation that refuses to obey the Lord its God, and refuses to be taught. She continues to live a lie.
>
> (Jeremiah 7:27,28 LB)

What about today? Is God once again warning that His wrath is about to fall in all its fury? Is the Holy Spirit of God warning true believers to "get their houses in order"? Are we living right now in the time Jesus described as "the beginning of sorrows"? Are we actually now seeing the "beginning of the end"? Is God once again sending to this, our drinking, revelling society, a final warning that "the party is over"? Positively yes! God has always warned His people just prior to the outpouring of judgment and calamity. Just before it happened, Noah was sent by God to warn all who would listen that the party was over and that a flood was coming.

God sent two angels, disguised as human prophets, to warn the righteous to flee from the twin cities of Sodom and Gomorrah because of the coming judgment. But in nearly every instance in history, God's merciful warnings have gone unheeded. The masses continued eating, drinking, marrying, divorcing, and feasting and "knew not until the flood came, and took them all away" (Matthew 24:39 KJV). One bright, sunny day while the Sodomite crowds went about indulging their lusts, fire bombs fell from Heaven and consumed them in a white-hot holocaust. It happened just as God warned it would.

13

4. America Will Be Judged Soon

The Bible predicts that in the last days "young men shall see visions" (Acts 2:17). The message I share with you in this book is only one of many proclaiming that judgment is coming. It is a message completely endorsed by predictions of Jesus Christ himself. It came to me in the secret closet of prayer, and like others who have seen things that are coming, I was frightened.

I see fearful judgments coming. They will not all come immediately, but I believe they will all take place in our generation. We are on the brink of divine judgments so severe not one person will be left untouched.

> I set watchmen over you who warned you: "Listen for the sound of the trumpet! It will let you know when trouble comes." But you said, "No! We won't pay any attention!"
>
> (Jeremiah 6:17 LB)

5. I Am Not a Jeane Dixon

Before I share this message let me give you some background. I do not consider myself a prophet and I have always been wary of visions, dreams, and impressions. I believe we get our directions from the Word of God, and I have always been Bible-centered in my preaching. We live in a time when astrologers, mentalists, fortune-tellers, and self-acclaimed prophets and prophetesses like Edgar Cayce and Jeane Dixon have acquired tremendous followings. But, ever since Moses' day, astrologers and soothsayers have had to stand back in awe when the "finger of God" appeared. That same finger of God appeared in the time of King Belshazzar, and no magician or soothsayer could interpret God's handwriting on the wall. The soothsayers, prognosticators, and astrologers of today are voicing nothing but echoes and shadows. Isaiah said of them:

14

You have advisors by the ton—your astrologers and stargazers, who try to tell you what the future holds. But they are as useless as dried grass burning in the fire. They cannot even deliver themselves! You'll get no help from them at all. Theirs is no fire to sit beside to make you warm!

(Isaiah 47:13,14 LB)

I know I have seen the appearance of the finger of God against this generation, too. My directions are simply to cry aloud and share these warnings in every way possible. I must urge people to "get their houses in order." I know people will call me an alarmist, a sensationalist, and a preacher of doom and despair. Critics will fault my methods, agnostics will mock the message, and even well-meaning ministers and church leaders will refute the message as "not from God"—even before they have shut themselves in the secret closet of prayer to see if these things really be true. Nevertheless, God's prophetic warnings will always stand the test of criticism, denial, and rejection. The greatest rejection will come from those who believe their vested interests are threatened. The purpose of any warning is to nudge God's children into the perfect center of His will and to prepare them for the coming crises. It is also God's way to justify the impending judgment. A just God sends forth merciful warnings of what He is about to do. God seeks to melt men in a crucible of affliction.

She indulged herself in immorality, and refused to face the fact that punishment was sure to come. Now she lies in the gutter with no one left to lift her out. "O Lord," she cries, "see my plight. The enemy has triumphed."

(Lamentations 1:9 LB)

6. Quit Preaching Doom

The party is definitely over and I get very weary of people who say to me, "Don't preach such gloom or you may help bring it to pass." Isaiah said: "They tell God's prophets, 'Shut up! We don't want any more of your gloom. Tell us nice things; we've had about enough of your sad reports' " (Isaiah 30:10,11 LB).

Noah's preaching did not bring the flood; God had already passed judgment. Isaiah's preaching and warning did not bring the invading armies into Judah and Jerusalem. The warnings of destruction by the two angels did not bring the fire upon Sodom. When the cup of iniquity is full, judgment is inevitable.

After the vision Isaiah received from God, he confessed, "I am gripped by an awful fear. I can no longer sleep, and lie awake, trembling" (Isaiah 21:4 LB).

The prophet Daniel received a vision that would affect the future of all mankind. He was so disturbed by the frightening word from God, he confessed, "When I awoke, I was greatly disturbed, and my face was pale with fright. Then I grew faint and was sick for several days" (Daniel 8:17,27 LB).

The Bible claims that conditions will become so terrifying that the number one killer in the world will be heart disease and "men's hearts shall fail them for fear for watching those things that are coming upon the earth" (Luke 21:26 LB).

All the institutions around us seem to be crumbling; government leaders are lying and cheating; and there is very little left in the world to trust. But it is for times like these the sure Word of the Lord has been given. All other ground around us may be sinking, but His Word is the solid rock.

7. America Is In Trouble

Noah's generation is gone. Sodom is gone. Nineveh is gone. Tyre is gone. Babylon is gone. The Grecian Empire is gone. The Roman Empire is gone. The British Empire is gone. And now, the United States of America has begun its slide into oblivion, just like all the others. They were all judged and humbled because of violence, godlessness, homosexuality, and pride.

The land we all love is in critical danger. That may anger you. That may cause your patriotic blood to boil. But that does not change the facts. Millions of dead men from all these destroyed nations and empires will rise on the day of judgment to rebuke this generation for refusing to learn by their mistakes. Be assured that our righteous God warned every fallen society. He sent His servants, rising early in the morning, to warn them judgment was near.

> And now, because ye have done all these works, saith the Lord, and I spake unto you, rising up early and speaking, but ye heard not; and I called you, but ye answered not. . . .

> Since the day that your fathers came forth out of the land of Egypt unto this day I have even sent unto you all my servants the prophets, daily rising up early and sending them.

> (Jeremiah 7:13,25 KJV)

2

Judgment on America

1. A Chain of Judgments

The judgments of God come in dreadful succession. They are linked together in a chain, each one connected to the other. His judgments are never haphazard. Natural forces become God's supernatural instruments of judgment.

Divine judgments always begin with "small commotions" of nature, which is God's way of pleading with mankind to repent. Then follow major crises, when His pleadings turn to protests. A God who is but little displeased is provoked to anger because of men rushing to judgment. "And I am very sore displeased with the heathen that are at ease: for I was but a little displeased, and they helped forward the affliction" (Zechariah 1:15 KJV).

God does not sit as an unconcerned spectator when judgment falls. It comes from His mind, by His hands. Judgment is God at work.

> The Lord replied: "Look, and be amazed! You will be astounded at what I am about to do! For I am going to do something in your own lifetime that you will have to see to believe."
>
> (Habakkuk 1:5 LB)

2. God Will Roar

Judgment is God's "roaring" against wickedness. And God sends watchmen with warnings to avert judgments, not just to announce them. God always hopes his warnings will be heeded and judgment avoided.

I believe this generation is already in the process of being judged. We have been to His court, we have lost our case, the penalty has been pronounced, and the execution of the sentence is already under way. We are in a pause just before judgment, because God is slow to anger and is merciful. He is giving mankind time and space to repent.

> For thou, Lord, art good, and ready to forgive; and plenteous in mercy unto all them that call upon thee.
>
> (Psalms 86:5 KJV)

That is why the Lord says, "Turn to me now, while there is time. Give me all your hearts. Come with fasting, weeping, mourning. Let your remorse tear at your hearts and not your garments." Return to the Lord your God, for he is gracious and merciful. He is not easily angered; he is full of kindness, and anxious not to punish you. Who knows? Perhaps even yet he will decide to let you alone and give you a blessing instead of a curse. Perhaps he will give you so much that you can offer your grain and wine to the Lord as before!

(Joel 2:12–14 LB)

3. The Suspended Specimen

The impending judgment will be just a specimen of the final judgment on all the earth. God's cup of wrath holds only so much iniquity. When it is full, it spills over. Judgment is nothing but sin ripened. It is a volcano that erupts at the point of unmanageable pressure. Sin is the fire, and the sinner becomes the fuel.

I believe judgment is "suspended" over the world at this very moment and will fall suddenly in a series of "black days." Society has developed a death wish. We are committing moral suicide. We are the authors of our own destruction. Our wounds are self-inflicted, and the result is moral madness. People go about putting on nooses, preparing themselves for hanging: "O Israel, thou hast destroyed thyself; but in me is thine help."

(Hosea 13:9 KJV)

4. Funeral Dirge

The funeral dirge has begun, and we are about to witness the mass burial of thousands who have betrayed the Lord God. Nothing can prop up the rotting foundations of this doomed society. Our world will cringe in fear at the awesome sight of massive death, destruction, and upheaval. Mankind is hemorrhaging with sin, and

19

the bleeding cannot be stopped. People now sin openly in the streets, no longer able to blush. Obsessed with wealth, dollars, and delicacies. God says, "It is your house now, and it's left to you desolate. Not mine anymore" (Luke 13:35). Our sin is now malignant and spreading.

Perhaps even yet they will turn from their evil ways and ask the Lord to forgive them before it is too late, even though these curses of God have been pronounced upon them.

(Jeremiah 36:7,8 LB)

5. God's Bow

Judgment is God's bow. The arrows are His divine instruments of wrath. And the only reason America has not yet been severely stricken is that God is bending the bow and pulling the string tighter. All the swifter and more deadly will be our judgment.

He bends his bow against his people as though he were an enemy. His strength is used against them to kill their finest youth. His fury is poured out like fire upon them.

(Lamentations 2:4 LB)

6. The False Boom

A wave of prosperity usually precedes great judgments. This is God's way of making one last appeal, through goodness rather than wrath. God pours on the good, the prosperity, hoping it will lead man to repentance.

Don't you realize how patient he is being with you? Or don't you care? Can't you see that he has been waiting all this time without punishing you, to give you time to turn from your sin? His kindness is meant to lead you to repentance.

(Romans 2:4 LB)

But man uses prosperity as a sign God is pleased. Mankind is doing just that. We justify our weaknesses by our successes. We seem to be saying, "We are rich and prosperous; we must be right." "Things are going so good, God must be well pleased."

> Because thou sayest, I am rich, and increased with goods, and have need of nothing; and knowest not that thou art wretched, and miserable, and poor, and blind, and naked.
>
> (Revelation 3:17 KJV)

When a society gets rich and prosperous, it becomes blinded to its spiritual bankruptcy. Yes, we are "rich and increased with goods, and have need of nothing." But the Bible says, "Riches profit not in the day of wrath" (Proverbs 11:4 KJV). A temporary boom is God's last "goodness call" to a forgetful society. In a time of prosperity, men forget God and provoke Him to come forth as a lion to destroy.

> So I will come upon you like a lion, or a leopard lurking along the road. I will rip you to pieces like a bear whose cubs have been taken away, and like a lion I will devour you.
>
> (Hosea 13:7,8 LB)

When? God will come forth as a lion to judge the unprepared in a time of "dwelling at ease" and "laying up goods." This nation wants perpetual comfort and never-ending pleasures. We have overestimated success and have become a nation of proud peacocks. Reason has given way to self-intoxication. And because success cultists cannot handle disappointments, this nation is terrified by the very thought of deprivation and sorrow.

7. All Escape Routes Cut Off

When judgment falls, God cuts off all avenues of evasion. All escape routes are cut off, because of the people's insensibility to sin. God begins to remove one support after another. One by one, trusted institutions begin to fail. Little by little, all that was once solid and sure begins to erode and disintegrate. Moral standards melt like snow. Consequently, men are then governed by their sensual appetites and not intelligence. Sin wraps itself in robes of piety so it can't be recognized. Sin grows bold, self-excusing, and runs unchecked because it lies hidden beneath the false fronts of dead religion. That makes evil men feel secure, causing those who are furthest from God to claim to be closest to Him.

> Therefore, the Lord says, I am going to bring calamity down upon them and they shall not escape. Though they cry for mercy, I will not listen to their pleas.
>
> (Jeremiah 11:11 LB)

8. Men Begin to Glory in Their Gore

This nation will be judged because it has begun to glory in its gore. Our nation is becoming stupefied by sin, blinded by brazenness, and crippled by corruption.

Our land will be judged for a "spirit of rejoicing in evil." Sinners no longer blush. They sin openly and brazenly and rejoice in their iniquity. They now pursue their wickedness with zest and enthusiasm, making their wickedness a source of laughter and rejoicing. We sing now about our sins.

> What right do my beloved people have to come any more to my Temple? For you have been unfaithful and worshiped other gods. Can promises and sacrifices now avert your doom and give you life and joy again?
>
> (Jeremiah 11:15 LB)

No other generation has rejoiced so much in evil practices. Homosexuals rejoice in their iniquity. They flaunt their lewdness and stand in God's house claiming to be "delivered" to indulge in their sins. "And come and stand before me in this house, which is called by my name, and say, 'We are delivered to do all these abominations' " (Jeremiah 7:10).

They refuse to change their ways, so instead they rejoice because of their weaknesses. The nation has become polluted with sinners accustomed to evil. They have lost all sense of guilt and have become comfortable in their sins. The rapist will soon be looked upon as heroic, the criminal will be applauded by the masses. The cheater and the adulterer will be looked upon as cunning and resourceful, for the ultimate end result of "rejoicing in iniquity" is the exaltation of the vile and lawless. These sinners and corrupters will be encouraged in their evil pursuits by permissive laws, compromising judges, and a sensuous society. Can God spare a nation from judgment that not only exalts sin but flaunts it in His face with a devilish spirit of rejoicing? No! God must judge this nation for becoming entrenched and satisfied with corruption.

> Can the Ethiopian change his skin, or the leopard his spots? Then may ye also do good, that are accustomed to do evil.
>
> (Jeremiah 13:23 KJV)

9. Prophets of the Positive

All the smiley bumper stickers cannot camouflage the sense of judgment upon the land. Our nation is being deluged with books, lectures, and predictions of prosperity and growth by men who call themselves "prophets of the positive," and they try to blunt the sharp edge of God's warnings about coming judgment, even quoting Scripture to their own advantage.

> Many will say to me in that day, Lord, Lord, have we not prophesied in thy name? and in thy

23

name have cast out devils? and in thy name done many wonderful works? And then will I profess unto them, I never knew you: depart from me, ye that work iniquity.

(Matthew 7:22,23 KJV)

They say, "Crime has always been bad, even in Socrates' time." They admit our planet is polluted, but they look to science to work a miracle of deliverance. They say, "Let's look on the bright side." They quote from Paul, who said, "Whatsoever things are pure, honest, and of good report, think on these things" (Philippians 4:8). Forgetting that Paul also warned, "For when [men] shall say, Peace and safety; then sudden destruction cometh upon them, as travail upon a woman with child; and they shall not escape" (1 Thessalonians 5:3 KJV). And that, too, is something to think about!

The surest sign of divine judgment is the appearance of so many false prophets predicting peace and prosperity. They are rising up all over the land, preaching false visions, dreams, and the deceits of their own hearts. Many of them are merchandisers who profit from their own predictions of "boom times" ahead.

They look into the future and see peace, prosperity, and abundance ahead. They prophesy what people want to hear. Any negative message angers them, and the only thing they can prophesy is peace, prosperity, and plenty.

Then said I, Ah, Lord God! behold, the prophets say unto them, Ye shall not see the sword, neither shall ye have famine; but I will give you assured peace in this place. Then the Lord said unto me, The prophets prophesy lies in my name: I sent them not, neither have I commanded them, neither spake unto them: they prophesy unto you a false vision and divination, and a thing of nought, and the deceit of their heart. Therefore thus saith the Lord concerning the prophets that prophesy in my

24

name, and I sent them not, yet they say, Sword and famine shall not be in this land; By sword and famine shall those prophets be consumed.

(Jeremiah 14:13–15 KJV)

Who are these false prophets? Are they occultists, witch doctors, or demon-possessed fanatics? No! The false prophets that now preach the worst deception are economists, government statisticians, politicians, experts, and slumbering shepherds.

As for my people, children are their oppressors, and women rule over them. O my people, they which lead thee cause thee to err, and destroy the way of thy paths.

(Isaiah 3:12 KJV)

God will allow them to be deceived and be deluded by lies. He will blind their eyes and send upon them helpless bewilderment. They will be the benign agents of Satan to deceive and mislead this wicked nation.

For thus saith the Lord of hosts, the God of Israel; Let not your prophets and your diviners, that be in the midst of you, deceive you, neither hearken to your dreams which ye cause to be dreamed.

(Jeremiah 29:8 KJV)

With distortions, false predictions, lying promises, they will lull the nation with a false sense of security. The president cries, "Away with doomsayers—they are wrong. See, all is turning out well. They are all wrong. Prosperity and peace are ahead." An army of experts, economists, and high officials go about the land now as commissioned prophets of optimism, prophesying a bright future. They are totally blinded to the warning signs all around. They are false prophets. People who believe their predictions are encouraged in their sins and are convinced that judgment is not coming. Reassuring words from these prophets of prosperity discourage repentance.

I have seen also in the prophets of Jerusalem an horrible thing: they commit adultery, and walk in lies: they strengthen also the hands of evildoers, that none doth return from his wickedness: they are all of them unto me as Sodom, and the inhabitants thereof as Gomorrah.

(Jeremiah 23:14 KJV)

Thus saith the Lord of hosts, Hearken not unto the words of the prophets that prophesy unto you: they make you vain: they speak a vision of their own heart, and not out of the mouth of the Lord. They say still unto them that despise me, The Lord hath said, Ye shall have peace; and they say unto every one that walketh after the imagination of his own heart, No evil shall come upon you. For who hath stood in the counsel of the Lord, and hath perceived and heard his word? Who hath marked his word, and heard it? Behold, a whirlwind of the Lord is gone forth in fury, even a grievous whirlwind: it shall fall grievously upon the head of the wicked. The anger of the Lord shall not return, until he have executed, and till he have performed the thoughts of his heart: in the latter days ye shall consider it perfectly. I have not sent these prophets, yet they ran: I have not spoken to them, yet they prophesied. But if they had stood in my counsel, and had caused my people to hear my words, then they should have turned them from their evil way, and from the evil of their doings.

(Jeremiah 23:16–22 KJV)

10. Horoscope, Witches, Mystics
This generation will be judged for indulging in heathen practices. Millions are turning to horoscopes and confi-

26

dence in the stars. People refuse the knowledge of God, yet seek after guidance and assurance from heathen signs. God is angered by the multitudes who trust not in Him but in foolish signs of the stars.

The wisdom of God is despised and rejected for the ridiculous advice of psychics, witches, and stargazers. A growing number of people put more confidence in their daily horoscope than they do in God's holy word. They conduct the course of their lives by the movement of stars. God has declared: ". . . the way of man is not in himself: it is not in man that walketh to direct his own steps" (Jeremiah 10:23).

The God who formed the world in His own wisdom and who controls the resources of all knowledge desires to be consulted and trusted. He said, "Call upon me, and I will answer" (Zechariah 13:9). Instead, millions of Americans call upon their psychics, their fortunetellers, their soothsayers. This is an act of open rebellion against God. These lying mystics preach the doctrine of vanity. They are all liars. They have no true wisdom or knowledge. They cannot decipher the finger of God. They cannot tap the treasures of divine wisdom. Their guidance is sensual, earthly, and destructive. They will all perish in judgment.

> Fortune-tellers' predictions are all a bunch of silly lies. . . .
>
> (Zechariah 10:2 LB)

> They are vanity, and the work of errors: in the time of their visitation they shall perish.
>
> (Jeremiah 10:15 KJV)

11. True Prophecy Rejected

God will judge this nation for turning a deaf ear to true prophecies of both deliverance and destruction. No nation on earth has been so blessed with men of God who have heard from Heaven. A gift of true prophecy has come

27

forth upon the land, upon young and old, and the word of the Lord has gone forth. God has heaped warning upon warning. From early morning to late at night, the airwaves are filled with trumpet calls, warnings, pleadings, beseechers and prophesiers. God has warned this nation in love, hoping and pleading for a people to seek Him and call upon Him for help.

> For I know the thoughts that I think toward you, saith the Lord, thoughts of peace, and not of evil, to give you an expected end. Then shall ye call upon me . . . and I will hearken unto you. And ye shall seek me, and find me, when ye shall search for me with all your heart.
>
> (Jeremiah 29:11–13 KJV)

The message of all the true prophets of the Lord has been the same as delivered to the prophet Jeremiah and his generation:

> . . . Do not provoke God to anger with the works of your hands; and He will do you no hurt . . . But if you will not hearken to the message of the Lord, and provoke Him to anger . . . the whole land will become a desolation and an astonishment. . . .
>
> (Jeremiah 25:6,7,11)

Judgment is coming soon because we have provoked God to anger by not heeding His warnings.

12. Refusing God's Hour of Visitation

God sends judgment when men reject their "hour of visitation." Jesus stood over Jerusalem weeping, because that city was about to fall under judgment for "knowing not the time of visitation."

> And when he was come near, he beheld the city, and wept over it, Saying, If thou hadst known, even thou, at least in this thy day, the things which

belong unto thy peace! but now they are hid from thine eyes. For the days shall come upon thee, that thine enemies shall cast a trench about thee, and compass thee round, and keep thee in on every side, And shall lay thee even with the ground, and thy children within thee; and they shall not leave in thee one stone upon another; because thou knewest not the time of thy visitation.

(Luke 19:41–44 KJV)

God poured out upon Jerusalem "a spirit of grace and supplication" (Zechariah 12:10). Christ had come, as all the prophets predicted He would, to bring everyone together in Himself. He came to anoint, to heal, to unite. He came to gather everyone together under His wings as a mother hen gathers together her chicks. But Jerusalem was blind to its hour of destiny. The religious leaders would have nothing to do with God's divine plan. Religious tradition kept the masses in blindness, so they could not discern the mighty work of God through Christ: "I sent my prophets to warn you with many a vision and many a parable and dream" (Hosea 12:10 LB).

Today, in our time, God has sent forth the Holy Spirit. This great outpouring was meant to be for our coming together in peace. God intended Irish Catholics to be one with Irish Protestants, through the Spirit. He intended that all American Christians come together at the cross! But the Spirit is being rejected by those in authority. There is official blindness in our "hour of visitation."

I sent my prophets to warn you of your doom; I have slain you with the words of my mouth, threatening you with death. Suddenly, without warning, my judgment will strike you as surely as day follows night.

(Hosea 6:5 LB)

13. Mercenary Missionaries

This nation will be judged for expanding its wickedness to the far corners of the earth. Like a whirlwind, we have spread our iniquities from nation to nation.

> Prostitutes charge for their services—men pay with many gifts. But not you, you give *them* gifts, bribing them to come to you! So you are different from other prostitutes. But you had to pay them, for no one wanted you. (Ezekiel 16:33,34 LB)

With bribery, cheating, and deceit, this nation has corrupted the innocent as well as the willing. Europe sends to our shores pornography, smut, and corrupt movies. America sends to Europe and the world a "spirit of deception." The rewarding of corruption through unlawful bribes is the sin of extortion that God must judge.

> Must I forever see this sin and sadness all around me? Wherever I look there is oppression and bribery and men who love to argue and to fight. The law is not enforced and there is no justice given in the courts, for the wicked far outnumber the righteous, and bribes and trickery prevail. (Habakkuk 1:3,4 LB)

America has made all the earth drink from its cup of iniquity. Once we were known for sending missionaries to deliver men and societies from the bondage of sin and corruption. We once sought to cover the nakedness and expel the darkness of undeveloped nations. Now America condones the nakedness and exports its own deeds of darkness. We bribe the world seeking favors.

> But no, my people are like crafty merchants selling from dishonest scales—they love to cheat. Ephraim boasts, "I am so rich! I have gotten it all by myself!" But riches can't make up for sin. (Hosea 12:7,8 LB)

Multinational corporations are the most popular missionaries of modern America. While Christ's missionaries are harassed and neglected through lack of funds and official government support, profit-obsessed corporations cover the earth preaching a gospel of materialism and extortion.

But now I snap my fingers and call a halt to your dishonest gain and bloodshed. How strong and courageous will you be then, in my day of reckoning? For I, the Lord, have spoken, and I will do all that I have said.

(Ezekiel 22:13,14 LB)

How can God but judge a nation that spends more money, time, and energy putting Coca-Cola instead of Bibles in the hands of all the earth's inhabitants? How can God not judge a nation that now protects and admires its merchants more than its missionaries?

This is what I am going to do: I will gather together all your allies—these lovers of yours you have sinned with, both those you loved and those you hated—and I will make you naked before them, that they may see you.

(Ezekiel 16:37 LB)

14. A Godly Nation Turns Ungodly

America was once a godly nation. In the Declaration of Independence, Jefferson wrote of life and liberty as gifts from God. Our fathers were all united under God. "In the name of God, Amen." was written above the first document drawn up by our new government. "In God we trust" appears on United States coins. Several of the first signers of our Constitution were graduates of the College of New Jersey (now Princeton University), a God-centered school. They were schooled by John Witherspoon, a minister of Christ's Gospel.

31

In the 1790s, revival fires spread throughout New England. Camp meetings sprang up over the land. New churches were planted and entire cities repented and turned to Christ. By 1810, the American Board of Commissioners for Foreign Missions was formed. The fire of God was spread throughout the world, with great missionary zeal. In less than fifteen years, our nation had five other mission boards in operation.

> Thus wast thou decked with gold and silver; and thy raiment was of fine linen, and silk, and broidered work; thou didst eat fine flour, and honey, and oil: and thou wast exceeding beautiful, and thou didst prosper into a kingdom. And thy renown went forth among the heathen for thy beauty: for it was perfect through my comeliness, which I had put upon thee, saith the Lord God.
>
> (Ezekiel 16:13,14 KJV)

Bible societies, Sunday school societies, the temperance society—all came out of these early American revivals. This godly environment gave birth to abolition, women's suffrage, health reform, and political integrity. Judges read and respected the Bibles placed in their courtrooms. Schools were bulwarks against atheism and deism. Drunkenness was deplored and divorce was unacceptable.

God planted America in good soil, with unlimited freedom to become a land where He would be praised and exalted. For a long while it lasted, and God kept His part of the bargain. He prospered and blessed, just as He promised. But our nation became weary in its well doing. And now, a TV commercial sums it all up: "We've come a long way." Yes! A long way from God, from truth, from our heritage.

Now we are a nation with hordes of uncaged rapists—a nation of intellectual emptiness and unbelief in the supernatural. A shaky government with low ethics—having now a form of godliness without the power of God. There is pandemic divorce and a breakdown of family life.

> The shew of their countenance doth witness against them; and they declare their sin as Sodom, they hide it not. Woe unto their soul! for they have rewarded evil unto themselves.
>
> (Isaiah 3:9 KJV)

This is a nation glutted with Bibles of every version, yet without the true knowledge of God. A nation whose airwaves are filled to capacity with TV and radio programs preaching repentance, yet failing to heed the message. A nation with crumbling morals in the midst of the greatest outpouring of God's Holy Spirit ever witnessed. A nation that has failed to fulfill its righteous purpose under God.

> Ah sinful nation, a people laden with iniquity, a seed of evildoers, children that are corrupters: they have forsaken the Lord, they have provoked the Holy One of Israel unto anger, they are gone away backward.
>
> (Isaiah 1:4 KJV)

15. Communism the Wrong Enemy

Communism has not been your real enemy, America! No! Your enemy is within. That enemy lurks on every street corner and parades around in the wicked minds of your wild men and women. The enemy is Satan, and communism is but one of his demonstrations of evil. God has a controversy with communism and will destroy it from the face of the earth at Armageddon.

But what can God do with the outbreak in America of blatant rebellion against righteousness and the cross? The war against the cross in America is of far more concern to God than our battle against communism.

33

Your country is desolate, your cities are burned with fire: your land, strangers devour it in your presence, and it is desolate, as overthrown by strangers.

(Isaiah 1:7 KJV)

Communism will not rule the world; only God will. Judgment from almighty God will blow away the Russian and Chinese Empires like so much sand.

Behold, the nations are as a drop of a bucket, and are counted as the small dust of the balance: behold, he taketh up the isles as a very little thing. . . . All nations before him are as nothing; and they are counted to him less than nothing, and vanity. . . . Yea, they shall not be planted; yea, they shall not be sown: yea, their stock shall not take root in the earth: and he shall also blow upon them, and they shall wither, and the whirlwind shall take them away as stubble.

(Isaiah 40:15,17,24 KJV)

America is not being judged for appeasing communism. No! It is being judged for appeasing its own sinful lusts. Judged for allowing sin to multiply so fast without raising a loud voice of dissent. Instead the wicked are exalted and the preverse are praised.

16. Cursed by Idleness

How did the multitudes come to love idleness so? A welfare system that provides all the comforts and pleasures even to men too proud, too full, to work. Idleness has made us the "sister of Sodom." Sodom's streets were filled with idle men, proud, sensuous, and fat! God said, "Enough." Welfare must be provided to the truly poor and needy, as Christ demands. But not to those unwilling to work.

Behold, this was the iniquity of thy sister Sodom, pride, fulness of bread, and abundance of

34

idleness was in her and in her daughters, neither did she strengthen the hand of the poor and needy. And they were haughty, and committed abomination before me: therefore I took them away as I saw good.

(Ezekiel 16:49,50 KJV)

17. Down with the CIA

An inevitable sign of judgment is the loss of national will and an unwillingness to defend against oncoming tides. Security systems are the first to fail, as in the days of King Belshazzar. While the leaders of the land, the business tycoons, the armed forces captains all drank and played, enemy armies were just outside the gate, unnoticed and undetected. No security guards, no spies, no warning system to let them know the enemy was diverting the river that protected them. Babylon's security system broke down in the final hours of the empire.

And I will make drunk her princes, and her wise men, her captains, and her rulers, and her mighty men: and they shall sleep a perpetual sleep, and not wake, saith the King, whose name is the Lord of hosts.

(Jeremiah 51:57 KJV)

Babylon was crushed because it lost its will to defend itself. Corrupted by ease and alcohol, the men became "as women" and sought only the comforts of home and the pleasures of the city. All defenses were broken down. She became weaker than her enemies: "Therefore shall her young men fall in the streets, and all her men of war shall be cut off in that day, saith the Lord" (Jeremiah 50:30 KJV).

Isn't this exactly what is happening right now? We have cut our intelligence forces to shreds. We will soon be unable to detect the enemy forces at our gates. We are becoming weaker than our enemies, and our will to defend is waning. Our armies have become soft and in-

35

dulgent. We have withdrawn to the comforts and pleasures of our "good life." As with Babylon, "our might has failed" (Jeremiah 51:30). And when a stronger nation realized it had become more powerful, and that an idle Babylon would not fight back, the Medes went on the attack. The Babylonian Empire was crushed.

> How long must this land of yours put up with all their goings on? Even the grass of the field groans and weeps over their wicked deeds! The wild animals and birds have moved away, leaving the land deserted. Yet the people say, "God won't bring judgment on us. We're perfectly safe!"
>
> (Jeremiah 12:4 LB)

3

Judgment Warnings

1. The Wategate Warning

Watergate was the judgment of God upon one man: "He hath put down the mighty from their seats, and exalted them of low degree" (Luke 1:52 KJV).

A President, flushed with pride because of the American landing on the moon, deplaned in Communist Rumania to proclaim over satellite television to the whole world that mankind needed "the spirit of Apollo." This suggestion that the world should bow to the idol of a false god was a form of pride God would not allow to go unanswered. A fall was certain.

> Pride goeth before destruction, and an haughty spirit before a fall.

> A man's pride shall bring him low: but honour
> shall uphold the humble in spirit.
>
> (Proverbs 16:18; 29:23 KJV)

Two weeks after the President returned from his lofty trip, the agony of Watergate began. Ever since, America has been a troubled nation racing towards judgment.

Watergate should have been a warning to this nation that if God judges one man because of pride, stripping him of dignity and a place in history, He will likewise judge the entire nation for its pride and godless arrogance: "For the day of the Lord of hosts shall be upon every one that is proud and lofty, and upon every one that is lifted up; and he shall be brought low" (Isaiah 2:12 KJV).

While this nation allows one man to have heaped upon himself the sins and blame of an entire government, God calls for personal responsibility. This nation has made its former president a scapegoat for its corporate sins. It is a whitewash to turn eyes away from the horrible crimes still lingering in government's high places. This wickedness still in high places cannot find atonement in the crucifixion of a fallen President. This is a proud nation that makes its nest in the stars and now seeks to conquer other planets. But God laughs at these attempts, and He will bring us down to the dust.

> Though thou exalt thyself as the eagle, and
> though thou set thy nest among the stars, thence
> will I bring thee down, saith the Lord.
>
> (Obadiah 4 KJV)

> . . . thou woundedst the head of the house of
> the wicked. . . .
>
> (Habakkuk 3:13 KJV)

2. The Solzhenitsyn Warning

Aleksandr Solzhenitsyn prophesied in London that Britain was now less significant than Uganda. He warned Britons they were being lulled into thinking "these Islands will never be blown sky-high." Europe, he said, was a collection of cardboard stage sets all bargaining to see how little could be spent for defense to leave more money for the comforts of life. He warned, ". . . Contemporary society is living on self-deception and illusions . . . people build rickety structures to convince themselves that there is no danger . . . public hypocrisy is thriving . . . and as democracy grows weaker and weaker, loses more ground, so the face of tyranny spreads throughout the globe . . . modern society is hypnotized . . . they have lost all sense of danger and cannot see what is moving swiftly toward them . . . nothing left but depleted arrows in the quiver."

> And they shall look unto the earth; and behold trouble and darkness, dimness of anguish; and they shall be driven to darkness.
>
> (Isaiah 8:22 KJV)

I wish every Christian minister in this hell-bent nation would heed Solzhenitsyn's most recent apocalyptic message:

> All of us are standing on the brink of a great historic cataclysm, a flood that swallows up civilization and changes whole epochs. We have become hopelessly enmeshed in our slavish worship of all that is pleasant, all that is comfortable, all that is material; we worship things, we worship products. . . .

This Russian refugee has more discernment about the coming judgment than the majority of God's shepherds. What an indictment:

> You have lost all sense of danger—you cannot even see what is coming swiftly towards you—you have sold out to comforts and materialism.

Has God turned away from busy, unconcerned shepherds to send us a prophet from behind Satan's iron curtain to warn us of coming judgment?

> And the destruction of the transgressors and of the sinners shall be together, and they that forsake the Lord shall be consumed.
>
> (Isaiah 1:28 KJV)

3. The Roman Warning

Rome was the great empire during Christ's ministry on earth. At first the empire was benevolent toward Christians. But when it discovered they swore allegiance to Christ instead of Caesar, they were persecuted. Christians were simple, modest, and moral. They refused to participate in the wild games and feasting of the indulgent Romans. Instead, they condemned them for their obsession with amusement and pleasure. Rome was being swept away by a preoccupation with sports, fancy foods imported from around the world, amusements, and sexual pleasures of all kinds.

As Rome became more wicked and vile, God began to judge the empire with famine, plague, floods, and calamity. The Romans blamed the judgments on Christians and began to throw them to the lions. Christians went underground into catacombs. The empire rejected Christ, and God gave it up to judgment. Rome fell, and a city that once claimed a population of more than four million inhabitants was destroyed with the empire.

> The day of judgment has come; the morning dawns, for your wickedness and pride have run their course and reached their climax—none of these rich and wicked men of pride shall live. All your boasting will die away, and no one will be left to bewail your fate.
>
> (Ezekiel 7:10,11 LB)

4. The British Warning

Remember the great British Empire? In the height of glory, Queen Victoria celebrated her sixtieth anniversary. Leaders of colonies from all over the earth were gathered in London. A Royal Navy fleet of nearly two hundred ships crowded the harbor. Proud government troops paraded by the thousands. The sun never set on this empire, and a mighty nation rode a crest of pomp and glory. But a prophet's voice was heard in that same day. Rudyard Kipling, a patriotic poet, wrote in "Recessional":

> God of our fathers, known of old,
>   Lord of our far-flung battle-line,
> Beneath whose awful hand we hold
>   Dominion over palm and pine—
> Lord God of Hosts, be with us yet,
> Lest we forget—lest we forget! . . .
>
> Far-called, our navies melt away;
>   On dune and headland sinks the fire:
> Lo, all our pomp of yesterday
>   Is one with Nineveh and Tyre!
> Judge of the Nations, spare us yet,
> Lest we forget—lest we forget!

It seemed unthinkable in those times that such an empire could ever disintegrate. Yet, we have lived to see that day. England is now crumbling. America is already plummeting in the same direction.

> Have you seen this? [he asked] Is it nothing to the people of Judah that they commit these terrible sins, leading the whole nation into idolatry, thumbing their noses at me and arousing my fury against them? Therefore I will deal with them in fury. I will neither pity nor spare. And though they scream for mercy, I will not listen.
>
> (Ezekiel 8:17,18 LB)

5. The Shiloh Warning

One of the most conclusive warnings of divine judgment is revealed in the seventh chapter of Jeremiah. Through this great prophet, God spoke these words to all generations: ". . . go now to my place which was in Shiloh, where I set my name at first, and see what I did to it for the wickedness of my people Israel" (Jeremiah 7:12).

God is saying to us, as he said to Israel, go back to Shiloh and learn from that example. You will see what I do to a nation and a people who forsake me. Shiloh is your warning. It was once my house, with my blessing on it. The fall of Eli's house is also the fall of Israel, and the fall of all others who refuse the warnings. "The lofty looks of man shall be humbled, and the haughtiness of men shall be bowed down, and the Lord alone shall be exalted in that day" (Isaiah 2:11 KJV)

Eli and the leaders of Israel were old, weary, and backslidden. Their sons gave themselves over to the devil. "They knew not the Lord . . . their sins were very great . . . anything their soul desired they took . . . they abhorred the service of God . . . they lay with the women that assembled at the door of the tabernacle . . . they made the Lord's people to transgress . . . they hearkened not to the voice of their fathers. . . ."

Parents refused to restrain their delinquent sons and daughters. Every man became a law unto himself, and everybody was busy getting "fat with the chiefest of all the offerings" (1 Samuel 2:29 KJV).

And the people shall be oppressed, every one by another, and every one by his neighbour: the child shall behave himself proudly against the ancient, and the base against the honourable.

(Isaiah 3:5 KJV)

A chosen people, planted in a good land, had polluted themselves. Shiloh, God's house, became a den of robbers and a place of corruption. Lip service and tradition were heaped upon halfhearted sacrifices.

God raised up a voice; Little Samuel. "And the Lord said to Samuel, Behold, I will do a new thing in Israel, at which both the ears of every one that heareth it shall tingle. . . . I will judge his house for ever for the iniquity which he knoweth; because his sons made themselves vile, and he restrained them not" (1 Samuel 3:11, 13 KJV).

By vision God pronounced doom on the house of Eli and the nation Israel, for "the word of Samuel came to all Israel." God declared specific judgment to happen all in one day: "And this shall be a sign unto thee, that shall come upon thy two sons . . . in one day they shall die . . ." (1 Samuel 2:34).

What a terrible day of judgment that was! The glory of the Lord departed and Ichabod was born. All the predictions of judgment came to pass in very short time.

> And the Philistines fought, and Israel was smitten, and they fled every man into his tent: and there was a very great slaughter; for there fell of Israel thirty thousand footmen. And the ark of God was taken; and the two sons of Eli, Hophni and Phinehas, were slain.
>
> (1 Samuel 4:10,11 KJV)

Is America modern Shiloh? Will the glory of the Lord depart from us, just as from Israel in the days of Eli? In one day God can spank this nation. In one day our glory can fade. In one day we could be driven to our knees. In one day we could go from first to last. God is saying, "Remember Shiloh."

6. The Nineveh Warning

This province lived without fear, strong and powerful, for over five hundred years. It was dreaded by nations everywhere for its power and fortifications. It was the queen city of the Assyrian Empire. It had once repented at the preaching of Jonah, but a new generation arose that became violent and wicked. So once again, God sent a prophet to warn of impending judgment. Jonah's was a message of mercy, Nahum's was a message of judgment.

Nineveh was secure, quiet, and well fortified against attack. It was a city of multitudes, a city of great renown. Because the city had once been spared God's wrath, the inhabitants thought of God as "slow to anger"! They satisfied their minds that God's slowness to act was insurance against judgment.

Nineveh, during the time of the prophet Nahum, began to disintegrate morally. Effeminacy and lust became rampant and weakened the will of the people. Patriotism vanished as men became lovers of themselves. They turned a deaf ear to leaders and priests. No one was willing to stand up for moral right. People began to hoard silver and gold and run about purchasing expensive items.

The city became totally demoralized in spirit, and a once proud and powerful empire edged to the brink of collapse. It had been known as "the Place of the Lion," and now it staggered like a wounded mongrel.

It is an irrefutable fact of history that God judged Nineveh, just as Nahum prophesied He would. Its military might was destroyed, its chariots burned in fire. All its resources were drained and given to others. Its foreign ambassadors were grounded and the empire lost all its world influence. The empire came tumbling down in judgment, and every inhabitant was silenced.

The Lord of Hosts was very angry with your fathers. But he will turn again and favor you if only you return to him. Don't be like your fathers were! The earlier prophets pled in vain with them to turn from all their evil ways. "Come, return to me," the Lord God said. But no, they wouldn't listen; they paid no attention at all. Your fathers and their prophets are now long dead, but remember the lesson they learned, that *God's Word endures!* It caught up with them and punished them. Then at last they repented. "We have gotten what we deserved from God," they said. "He has done just what he warned us he would."

(Zechariah 1:2–6 LB)

The prophet Nahum gave five reasons why God had to send judgment on that society:

1. It had become bloody, violent, full of lies and robbery.
2. It was full of witchcraft, adultery, nakedness, and perversion.
3. Men became as women, and multitudes turned to drunkenness.
4. There was a loss of leadership, with captains like grasshoppers.
5. The ministers were slumbering, leaving the population crippled, void, and bruised.

Look again at the reasons why God destroyed Nineveh. This nation of ours is guilty of all five of these indictments. How can we escape judgment for doing the same things that destroyed Nineveh?

For if the word spoken by angels was stedfast, and every transgression and disobedience received a just recompence of reward; How shall we escape, if we neglect so great salvation; which at the first began to be spoken by the Lord, and was confirmed unto us by them that heard him. . . .

(Hebrews 2:2,3 KJV)

7. The Commission on Critical Choices Warning

The Commission on Critical Choices for Americans is a group of forty-two prominent Americans formed by Nelson Rockefeller. It recently published twelve volumes of studies and essays about national problems, at a cost of four million dollars. After four million dollars and years of study, what have forty-two of our best minds come up with? Ten pessimistic conclusions, as I interpret their findings:

1. "Experts have been talking gibberish all along."
2. "All we can do is try to understand our confusion."
3. "Our guideposts for social policy are schizophrenic."
4. "Spending more and more money to alleviate frustrations has gone too far."
5. "We are in a muddle about what to do concerning crime."
6. "The world is now so insane even abnormal persons are considered sane."
7. "No one can be sure he is sane and not a fool whistling in the dark."
8. "There are now doubts about the worth of children and the legitimacy of the family."
9. "A wave of antischool feeling shows our educational scheme is a failure."
10. "Hopes for education are overblown, and our hopes of changing man by changing his environment are dying."

These men have no prescription for healing! Refusing to accept the fact we are in a state of collapse, they call it a "state of pause." We have handed the future of this nation over to the experts, and they have miserably failed. Now they are forced to recognize that there is evil as well as good. And that man needs a faith in someone outside himself.

We can no longer distinguish between the sane and the insane. Since we refuse to accept guilt, we blame all our problems on "society." We have no more solutions, only "tolerable nonsolutions."

> The Lord of hosts hath purposed it, to stain the pride of all glory, and to bring into contempt all the honourable of the earth.
>
> (Isaiah 23:9 KJV)

4

The Flash Points of Judgment

What are the flash points of divine judgment? At what exact moment does God move against a people or a nation for their iniquity? Are there clues God has left in His trail of past judgments? Can we pinpoint the approximate hour of the outpouring of wrath by reading "the signs of our times"? What final slap in God's face triggers judgment? Is it possible to really *know* judgment is about to fall? Or, is it just a bunch of educated guesses and vague prophecies?

> Must I forever see this sin and sadness all around me? Wherever I look there is oppression and bribery and men who love to argue and to fight. The law is not enforced and there is no justice given in the courts, for the wicked far outnumber the righteous, and bribes and trickery prevail.
>
> (Habakkuk 1:3,4 LB)

There are very definite causes that precipitate divine judgment. In other words, when a nation repeats the mistake of past generations, it is judged at the same points for the same causes. I refer to them as flash points. This means the same judgments that fell on Sodom can be repeated. God promised to never again judge the earth with an overflowing flood, but He still has "reserves of fire" to try the earth.

> Therefore as I live, saith the Lord of hosts, God of Israel, Surely Moab shall be as Sodom, and the children of Ammon as Gomorrah, even the breeding of nettles, and saltpits, and a perpetual desolation. . . .
>
> (Zephaniah 2:9 KJV)

God must send judgment to America because this nation has reached every flash point which historically brought destruction to all past societies.

The Bible lists a number of flash points that bring on judgment. Let me bring six of them to your attention.

1. Putting Our Foot in God's Tent

God sends His powerful judgments immediately after mankind attempts *one step out of his assigned domain.* God put boundaries on mankind, the earth and its fullness. He was commanded to replenish and rule the earth. But, the universe is His. He calls every star by name!

David said, "The heavens are thine, the work of thy fingers, the moon and the stars, which thou hast ordained . . ." (Psalms 8:3). The prophet Isaiah said God "stretched out the heavens, and spread out a tent to dwell in . . . He created all these things. . . ."

> It is he that sitteth upon the circle of the earth, and the inhabitants thereof are as grasshoppers; that stretcheth out the heavens as a curtain, and spreadeth them out as a tent to dwell in. . . .
>
> (Isaiah 40:22 KJV)

When American astronauts landed on the moon and stepped off the Apollo craft, Commander Armstrong proudly announced, "One giant step for mankind." He simultaneously pronounced this nation's flash point of divine judgment. Foolish conjecture? Absolutely not. Pride is the sin of altitude. We usurp God's power by flying our puny little kites under His nostrils in impudence. "Who shall bring me down to the ground?" (Obadiah 3 KJV).

Remember the Tower of Babel? Mankind attempted the first step into the heavens. They said, "Let us build a tower . . . to reach into the heavens . . ." (Genesis 11:4). At that point, God immediately sent judgment. Confusion reigned and God said, "Enough."

Remember also Babylon and its precise hour of divine judgment? Isaiah said to that proud nation, "Thy pomp is brought down to the grave . . . thou art fallen from heaven . . . thou are cut down to the ground . . . for thou hast said in thine heart, *I will ascend into heaven . . . I will exalt my throne above the stars of God . . . I will ascend above the heights of the clouds* . . . yet thou shalt be brought down to hell . . ." (Isaiah 14:13–15 KJV).

Babylon attempted a giant step for mankind into the forbidden realm of pride and human arrogance. And God said, "Enough." God brought down this proud and powerful nation the moment a move was made to put its foot into "God's tent in the heavens."

I truly believe this nation reached the flash point of judgment when our spaceships landed on God's moon! Science paraded like a victor over the universe. Probes were announced into the vast reaches of the galaxy. God was brought lower and mankind was exalted higher. A victory for science. But look what has happened since the moon landing. A President who basked in the pride of the event fell from his high place. Never has the world witnessed such swift judgment, so complete and humiliating. But following that, our nation has experienced wave after wave of confusion, recession, violence, and corruption. And now we stand on the brink of the same judgment that fell on Babylon. Unless we truly repent, God will humble this nation, and it will be left weak and frail just like all the other nations that have forgotten God.

> All they shall speak and say unto thee, Art thou also become weak as we? art thou become like unto us? . . . For the Lord of hosts hath purposed, and who shall disannul it? and his hand is stretched out, and who shall turn it back?
>
> (Isaiah 14:10,27 KJV)

It is true that God is everywhere. I do not believe in a three-story universe with God and heaven upstairs, the earth in the middle and hell downstairs. And, I do not have a negative reaction to scientific advances. But I am fully convinced that our landing on the moon and space probing represents man's secret desire to "be as gods." Our space program is not based on a desire to get nearer to God, but an attempt to prove man's intellectual superiority over religious superstition.

There may be many godly people involved in the space program, but they do not set the policy nor do they fully understand the implications of what they are involved in.

Billions of dollars have been spent to invade the universe while millions suffer and die of starvation here on earth. Don't tell me God will allow this to go unanswered. The commandment of God to all men was to go to the poor and needy. The commandment has been broken, and that in itself is enough to bring God's anger to a flash point.

It would have been more accurate for Commander Armstrong to announce to the world, "One giant step toward judgment."

> The pride of thine heart hath deceived thee, thou that dwellest in the clefts of the rock, whose

habitation is high; that saith in his heart, Who shall bring me down to the ground? Though thou exalt thyself as the eagle, and though thou set thy nest among the stars, thence will I bring thee down, saith the Lord.

(Obadiah 3,4 KJV)

2. The Porno Plague

God sends judgment at the point sin becomes so flaunted and violent it "cries out" to be destroyed.

God sent judgment on Sodom and Gomorrah because their sin became so defiant and progressive it demanded swift action.

So the Lord told Abraham, 'I have heard that the people of Sodom and Gomorrah are utterly evil, and that everything they do is wicked. I am going down to see whether these reports are true or not. Then I will know.'

"What relatives do you have here in the city?" the men asked. "Get them out of this place—sons-in-law, sons, daughters, or anyone else. For we will destroy the city completely. The stench of the place has reached to heaven and God has sent us to destroy it."

(Genesis 18:20,21; 19:12,13 LB)

Homosexuals became so brazen they attempted to indulge their lusts upon the sacred and holy. Sexual deviation became suddenly violent, dangerous, and bloody. No one was safe walking the streets. The masses had given themselves over to bizarre sexuality. The sounds of depravity became so loud they began to "cry out"—total and final debauchery. When men "declare their sin as Sodom, and hide it not," they bring upon themselves sin's own reward. God said, "Enough."

The violent sins of America now cry for judgment. In

our day, homosexuals once again profane that which is holy and sacred. Our sexual behavior has become like Sodom's—violent, bizarre, and bloody. It is not safe to walk our streets. Rapists, sex maniacs, and sadists haunt our cities and towns. Our nation has become just like Sodom. There are thousands now who are so perverted they would attack angels on any street corner, if given the chance.

The cry of our sins has reached the throne of God. God has said, "Enough." Judgment has already been pronounced on the depraved, and God's messengers go up and down the land warning "sinners, Prepare; flee the wrath of God; judgment is coming."

Will God not judge a nation that allows its men to parade the streets strutting like peacocks in women's clothing? How long will God permit the perverted to rape, murder, molest, and prey on the innocent? How much longer can God permit smut, demon-inspired perversions, and sadistic films to break out unchecked? The nation is stung by this overwhelming baptism of filth—its courts are helpless and timid, its leaders afraid to act, and its righteous people lethargic. All the restraints are fading. Guilt is disappearing. And we have become worse than Sodom without even knowing how it happened.

God looks down from heaven, searching among all mankind to see if there is a single one who does right and really seeks for God. But all have turned their backs on him; they are filthy and with sin—corrupt and rotten through and through.

(Psalms 53:2,3 LB)

The United States of Sodom

America is right now totally diseased with the plague of pornography. Moral standards are in complete disarray. In fact, the United States will soon be the porno capital of the world. America has become Satan's dumping ground for the dregs from hell. Over 780 theaters show X-rated movies now on a regular basis, including the so-called high-class ones in our most sophisticated suburbs. Even in our smallest cities there are grubby sex-book stores, 8mm peep shows, massage parlors, and strip joints. These "temptation zones" were once contained in large cities, in the most rundown sections. Nowadays, America is so deep into Satan's porno plague, an avalanche is under way coast to coast. Walk into almost any newsstand, anywhere in the nation, and your mind gets a mud bath. America's sexual-media madness makes this nation far more corrupted than Sodom. They had no glossy sex magazines, no X-rated movies, no dirty television programming.

Try to tell me America is not another Sodom, and I'll tell you: that is premeditated ignorance. The shadow of Sodom looms over our whole society.

If the Lord of Hosts had not stepped in to save a few of us, we would have been wiped out as Sodom and Gomorrah were.

(Isaiah 1:9 LB)

The Two-Billion-Dollar Slap in God's Face

Smut has mushroomed into a two-billion-dollar-a-year crime-infested industry. While the church and the courts retreat and sit around in fear, Mafia allies are waging a full-scale war on decency and righteousness. Porno now invades every segment of this corrupted society.

What have we come to in America when an admitted former prostitute, Xaviera Hollander, sells nine million books boasting about her immorality? When *Playboy* magazine displays a cover with scenes of women masturbating? When topless chauffeurs whisk tourists in black Cadillacs from fancy hotels to sleazy massage parlors? When male hustlers stand on street corners, pouncing on passersby just as in Sodom? When sex becomes humiliating, filthy, and violent? When slick, expensive porno magazines, subscribed to even by ministers, carry articles and scenes on "how to make love to animals"? When bookstands carry brazen magazines on bestiality and sex with children? When San Francisco, the dirt capital of America, cannot prosecute a single smut pusher since 1971? When an influential university like Brandeis honors men who publish and distribute bizarre smut? When one company can gross over half a million dollars a year marketing whips, chains, and bondage devices for homosexuals and sadists? When "Midnight Blue," a three-times-a-week cable program in New York City, can run pornographic films in our nation's most populated city? When more and more cities now show X-rated movies on TV after midnight? When *Vogue* magazine can feature a twelve-page fashion spread showing a man beating up the model for gratification? When rape scenes are glorified and sadomasochists are allowed to roam the streets in search of victims?

> They are all adulterers; as a baker's oven is constantly aflame—except while he kneads the dough and waits for it to rise—so are these people constantly aflame with lust.
>
> (Hosea 7:4 LB)

The American "Right" to Perversion

How can God delay His judgment on a nation that defends pornography as a "right"? Recently, liberal First Amendment defenders rushed to the defense of an X-rated film, *Sweet Movie,* that featured a striptease for children, intercourse plus murder on a bed of sugar, vomiting and defecating adults who urinate on one another, all to the music of Beethoven's Ninth Symphony.

A recent issue of *Penthouse* featured a thirteen-page montage of sadomasochistic scenes, including a female sadist stabbing her lover's eye out with her spiked heels. Other popular X-rated movies now feature torture, murder, and devilish mutilations.

America has degenerated so fast even the most permissive liberals are becoming frightened. They were the ones who put out studies suggesting smut is just an innocent escape valve. They pushed their intellectual findings on an intimidated Congress and Supreme Court, calling for the abolition of all "puritan standards." Well, they got their wish, and now it's payday!

> Your deeds won't let you come to God again, for the spirit of adultery is deep within you, and you cannot know the Lord.
>
> (Hosea 5:4 LB)

Sexual Morons

Did the wave of smut lessen American hangups? Did it make this nation more healthy, with fewer sexual problems? Never! We have become a nation of sexual morons, with homosexuals and sadists who feel so liberated they can abuse the rest of society. The experts have succeeded in making deviates comfortable in their sins, convincing them they are normal and should not seek help. Consequently, we now live in a nation in which homosexuals can proudly boast, "We are the right ones; the rest of society is wrong."

> . . . your daughters turn to prostitution and your brides commit adultery. But why should I punish them? For you men are doing the same thing, sinning with harlots and temple prostitutes. Fools! Your doom is sealed, for you refuse to understand.
>
> (Hosea 4:13–14 LB)

The most significant development in America's new sexual freedom is the fact that sadomasochists, filled with aggression and hostility, go about searching for victims. Is this not the very same thing that happened in Sodom? Sadomasochists stormed the home of Lot to make rape victims of two visiting angels. What now threatens to tear our society apart actually precipitated swift judgment on Sodom. This unleashing of sexual hostility and violence against the pure and innocent in America has already passed the flash point. It can no longer be contained. All hope is gone for the healing of this plague: "For the sin of my people is greater than that of Sodom, where utter disaster struck in a moment without the hand of man" (Lamentations 4:6 LB).

The Warren court opened the floodgates of smut in 1966. Now, a decade later, the flood has so enveloped America that obscenity sits as king! And to think that even ministers testified in that Warren court that pornography had redeeming qualities under certain conditions.

> The shepherds of my people have lost their senses. . . .
>
> (Jeremiah 10:21 LB)

The Moral Landslide

In 1815, America still blushed at smut and pornography. In that year, six Philadelphians were convicted of displaying an indecent painting. In 1842, our courts banned the importing of smut. In 1865, our nation even made it unlawful to use the mail for the peddling of filth.

The moral landslide actually began in the early 1950s when *Lady Chatterley's Lover* became a best seller. The

Roth decision in 1957 was the key that opened the door for the uncontrolled tide of obscenity.

In the year in which we now live, anything goes. The courts have left it up to local communities to deal with pornography. But the communities are now so corrupt and intimidated by the wave of immodesty, nothing is done. The few who still fight against this flood are hampered by disinterested, backslidden judges. The onrushing hordes of porno pushers are bold and militant.

And where are the Christians? Why can't they rise up against these evildoers? I have the answer, and I am sure of it: God has already set the day of judgment, and His Spirit is restraining the righteous. Porno lovers and pushers are blind, headed for the ditch, and God has said, "Leave them alone to face their judgment."

Ephraim is joined to idols: let him alone.

Let them alone: they be blind leaders of the blind. And if the blind lead the blind, both shall fall into the ditch.

(Hosea 4:17 KJV)
(Matthew 15:14 KJV)

3. Vendetta and Violence

God judges a nation or a people at the very point it turns to violence. God hates violence, and every generation that has clothed itself with violence has been destroyed. Judgment is "the vengeance of the Lord" against man's violence. Israel reached the flash point of judgment when they "polluted themselves with blood" (Lamentations 4:14 KJV).

Violence that expresses itself in the shedding of innocent blood is the final indignity against God.

Ezekiel prophesied against Jerusalem as "that bloody city," a boiling pot covered over with scum. He said, "For this cause God shall send on you His fury" (Ezekiel 24:6).

God destroyed the earth in Noah's time because of violence. His pure eyes could no longer stand the sight of bloody violence, killing, and murder.

Meanwhile, the crime rate was rising rapidly across the earth, and, as seen by God, the world was rotten to the core. As God observed how bad it was and saw that all mankind was vicious and depraved, he said to Noah, "I have decided to destroy all mankind; for the earth is filled with crime because of man. Yes, I will destroy mankind from the earth."

(Genesis 6:11–13 LB)

Any honest American knows what is happening to this beautiful nation. It is being overrun with violence, rape, murder. Bloody gang rioting and senseless killing is erupting once again. Television is so corrupt and violent, it is a wonder God has been as patient as He has. The airwaves are filled with crime and detective stories featuring stabbings, beatings, murder, shootings, and endless scenes of bloodshed and violent death.

God's indictment of America is clear! "You eat the bread of wickedness, and drink the wine of violence" (Proverbs 4:17).

Violence has become the food of this society that feeds its lust on blood and killing. The Bible says, ". . . the transgressors shall eat violence" (Proverbs 13:2). Sinners eat it up. They love those programs on television that feature blood, guts, and killing. Anything less than that is too tame for the American public. We have a generation that has grown up feasting on this garbage. Violence is the rod of destruction that has been placed in the hand of the now generation. "Violence is risen up into a rod of wickedness . . ." (Ezekiel 7:11 KJV).

Uncontrolled violence has brought down every society from Noah's day to Hitler's Germany. Now it threatens modern America. We have not only reached this flash point of judgment, we have passed it.

> You swear and lie and kill and steal and commit adultery. There is violence everywhere, with one murder after another. That is why your land is not producing; it is filled with sadness, and all living things grow sick and die; the animals, the birds, and even the fish begin to disappear.
>
> (Hosea 4:2,3 LB)

4. Drunkenness

Alcohol has become the most powerful "false prophet" of this generation. Wine has created a nation of mockers who want to turn America into one big "happiness hour." Recently, I have discovered that growing numbers of once—dedicated Christians have turned to social drinking. They are becoming mockers of righteousness. "Wine is a mocker . . ." (Proverbs 20:1 KJV).

America has "erred through wine," making mistakes in judgment and discernment. Wine is not a lonely sin, it is the grandparent of a whole catalog of national corruptions.

Wine and whiskey produce weakness in a nation. They make members of society insensitive to danger. They cause condemned men to fall asleep in the very hour of doom. Drinking is America's number one problem in this judgment hour: "She indulged herself in immorality, and refused to face the fact that punishment was sure to come. Now she lies in the gutter . . ." (Lamentations 1:9 LB).

With cocktail in hand, our women sacrifice themselves on the altars of fashion. They give themselves up to the pursuit of ambition and fame.

Alcohol-crazed men desecrate our Scriptures, our sermons, and our Sundays. I am also fully convinced that America's plunge into alcoholism has perverted our judicial system. Laws are broken and our society slackens its concern for order and justice. When law loses its authority, judgment is near. Law is the soul of the land. We are now witnessing a massive "heart attack" in America, a coronary of the law.

We seem powerless to stop a flood of weak, perverted laws put upon society as a burden by corrupt, wine-sodden judges. "The law is not enforced and there is no justice given in the courts, for the wicked far outnumber the righteous, and bribes and trickery prevail" (Habakkuk 1:4 LB).

Drunkenness has caused Americans to feed their vanity and pamper their lusts. It causes sinners to become brutes who seek to overthrow the righteous. It turns men into moral pests. "Wine, women, and song have robbed my people of their brains" (Hosea 4:11 LB).

We seem to be acting like passengers on the *Titanic* who say, "If we go down, at least we go down in style, happy and stoned." That is why this nation goes about "walking in the counsels and the imaginations of their own disobedient minds."

Drunkenness has turned us into a "treacherous" people. We suffer a national hypocrisy that hunts down the sins in others while sheltering the same sins in ourselves.

Men who practice hate now cry out, "We need more love."

Men who are lazy and shiftless now scream, "We have lost our will to work."

Men who are hypocrites and liars cry, "We have become two-faced and cheap."

Men who play with secret sins preach, "We need more holiness."

Men who break the Commandments say, "Carry and sell more Bibles."

Alcohol has changed many ministers into mercenaries. Prophets have become hirelings. Meek men have become covetous. Brothers betray brothers, and the loyal become traitors. Fathers turn against sons, and a man's worst enemies are those of his own house. It has brought upon this nation deprivation and lust, and has been the breeder of every conceivable debauchery.

> The men of Israel finish up their drinking bouts, and off they go to find some whores. Their love for shame is greater than for honor. Therefore, a mighty wind shall sweep them away; they shall die in shame, because they sacrifice to idols.
>
> (Hosea 4:18,19 LB)

5. An Emphasis on Personhood!

The modern emphasis on personhood has nearly destroyed parenthood. America will now be judged because, according to the Bible, it is no longer a "keeper of homes" (Habakkuk 2:5).

Many homes have become a prison for discontented women, adulterous husbands, and disrespectful children. God hates divorce, and yet America now has a pandemic divorce rate. This next year, one million new divorces are projected. This means ten million more children of broken homes. What a national tragedy.

> For the Lord, the God of Israel, says he hates divorce and cruel men. Therefore control your passions—let there be no divorcing of your wives.
>
> (Malachi 2:16 LB)

Muddled Marriages

Marriage is a lock with God holding the key. Divorce is called treachery by God, and no nation can long exist without divine judgment when the very foundations crumble.

Eve, the first woman, projected herself into the pride of personhood. She despised her role, disregarded her position, and willfully broke the commandments that were given to produce a strong parenthood. Adam and Eve were judged immediately.

America has become a nation of neuters. A neuter is a creature with two minds, two egos, two bodies. It is called bisexual by moderns. This madness of sexual neutrality is the direct result of reversed roles. Men seek to be effeminate, and women try to be masculine.

If the foundations be destroyed, what can the righteous do?

(Psalms 11:3 KJV)

Neuters

According to biblical prophets, one of the most significant flash points of judgment is "when your men become as women." It seems we now have multitudes who say, "Don't call me male or female, call me *person*." Tragically, this emphasis on personhood has created a generation of neurotics with no respect for God-ordained roles.

Runaway Mothers

America's bicentennial year yielded a tragic statistic. More mothers than teenagers ran away from home. Many thousands of housewives just packed up and left, running from responsibility, children, and husbands. They have been so mind-programmed by the media they think it is the acceptable thing to do. They run away without shame or remorse.

I listen to their conversation and what do I hear? Is anyone sorry for sin? Does anyone say, "What a terrible thing I have done"? No, all are rushing pell-mell down the path of sin as swiftly as a horse rushing to the battle!

(Jeremiah 8:6 LB)

There are now thirteen thousand commercial day-care centers profiting from working mothers. Many are just human warehouses where children are simply stored without the love and attention of a caring father or mother. A few day-care centers are excellent and necessary. But, children, for too many parents, have become a burden. They feel "tied down" by kids.

How can God hold off judging a nation that allows so many of its children to be neglected, abandoned, abused, and made to feel unwanted? No wonder the Bible warns the day will come when a man's worst enemy will be they of his own house. These unwanted, abused children will soon rise up into an army of bitter youth ready to settle the account through betrayal.

> For death has crept in through your windows into your homes. He has killed off the flower of your youth. Children no longer play in the streets; the young men gather no more in the squares.
>
> (Jeremiah 9:21 LB)

The Big I and the Little You

The motto of many modern Americans is "A big I and a little you." And that is nothing but stinking pride. It has become a stench in God's nostrils. Everyone appears to be looking out for self. The attitude is "get all you can, while you can. If anyone gets hurt, it's his own fault."

A strong society is based on Christ's concept that we are all servants, called to humbly assist our brothers and sisters. Too many Americans have scuttled that concept. Today, it is "I am my own person, make room—get out of my way—I know my rights."

That is the flash point of judgment!

> When pride cometh, then cometh shame . . . the perverseness of transgressors shall destroy them. (Proverbs 11:2,3 KJV)

6. The Sign of Jonah

Jesus was asked by His disciples, "When shall the end come? What signs or clues should we look for?" Christ not only answered them, he answered us at the same time. We have been given one final, totally conclusive sign that reveals the flash point of judgment:

> A wicked and adulterous generation seeketh after a sign; and there shall no sign be given unto it, but the sign of the prophet Jonas [Jonah]."
>
> (Matthew 16:4 KJV)

This prophetic message of Christ is a dual prophecy. First, just as Jonah, Christ was in the heart of the earth for three days. He was resurrected and came forth preaching mercy and judgment. Jonah preached to Nineveh, Christ preaches to this generation.

But an even more significant prophecy is intended. Christ is saying, "When you see your society once again becoming wicked and corrupt like Nineveh, and when Jonahs once again appears on your streets warning of impending judgment, you can know the day of reckoning has come."

> For as Jonas [Jonah] was a sign unto the Ninevites, so shall also the son of man be to this generation.
>
> (Luke 11:30 KJV)

Nineveh II

Is that why there are now thousands of young men and women standing on street corners of nearly every city in America preaching judgment? It is like an underground army. They have no organization, but they all preach the same message: "Prepare! This wicked nation is about to be judged."

God loves America just as much as He loved Nineveh. And God refuses to judge a society until "Jonah has had his day in the streets." It is Nineveh all over again. It is Jonah all over again. And if America rejects, it will be judgment all over again.

The men of Nineveh shall rise in judgment with this generation, and shall condemn it: because they repented at the preaching of Jonas and, behold, a greater than Jonas is here.

(Matthew 12:41 KJV)

5

The Punishment of America

Is God deaf and blind—he who made ears and eyes? He punishes the nations—won't he also punish you? He knows everything—doesn't he also know what you are doing?

(Psalms 94:9,10 LB)

America is right now racing toward judgment. Already this nation is facing punishment for its horrible sin and debauchery. We are experiencing only "the beginning of sorrows," but soon the entire nation will drink of God's cup of wrath.

But soon unheard-of terror will fall on them. God will scatter the bones of these, your enemies. They are doomed, for God has rejected them.

(Psalms 53:5 LB)

I believe God is going to judge this nation with three instruments of destruction. They are earthquakes, droughts, and financial disasters. Every nation God has judged in the past was "appointed" special instruments of calamity. Jeremiah the prophet warned his people of four kinds of disaster coming as judgment against sin.

> And I will appoint over them four kinds, saith the Lord: the sword to slay, and the dogs to tear, and the fowls of the heaven, and the beasts of the earth, to devour and destroy.
>
> (Jeremiah 15:3 KJV)

1. Killer Earthquakes

I believe God has appointed the instrument of killer earthquakes as His most ominous weapon of judgment. Our nation will undoubtedly suffer the most severe judgment of all. It will strike suddenly, without warning. God has forewarned through many prophetic messages. Even scientists have been warning that major quakes are coming. It will not come as a surprise. The very first tremor will send forth the judgment message loud and clear to all— THIS IS IT! A day of judgment has come! There are no words in our language to describe the horror and the suffering. There will be no way of escape. The worst that man feared will suddenly come upon him.

God will literally shake our nation with this instrument of judgment. The mountains will tremble and the cities will fall. "Quakerproof" buildings will crumble like sand castles. Power lines will crack like toothpicks. The earth will heave, split apart, and tremble.

> And they shall go into the holes of the rocks, and into the caves of the earth, for fear of the Lord, and for the glory of his majesty, when he ariseth to shake terribly the earth.
>
> (Isaiah 2:19 KJV)

Hundreds of Square Miles Affected

In less than two minutes on God's judgment clock, the death angel will claim the lives of multiplied thousands over a radius of hundreds of miles. Mountain-pass roads of escape will be blocked. Water mains will crumble and break. Cars and houses will sway like toys tossed about. Dams will burst and flood tides will carry many to their doom.

Those who lived sumptuously, carelessly, so unconcerned, will suddenly find themselves being entombed in quaking valleys of death. Transportation will cease in a moment of time. No buses. No trains. No planes. No cars. Roads twisted or covered with tons of broken overpasses.

> Fear, and the pit, and the snare, are upon thee, O inhabitant of the earth. And it shall come to pass, that he who fleeth from the noise of the fear shall fall into the pit; and he that cometh up out of the midst of the pit shall be taken in the snare: for the windows from on high are open, and the foundations of the earth do shake.
>
> (Isaiah 24:17,18 KJV)

Most Destructive in History

The Guatemala earthquake was small in comparison. The earthquake in Alaska cannot compare. This earthquake could be the most destructive in the world's history in overall total evaluations. The damage may never be measured in dollar value—ever. And when it strikes, the nation and the world will tremble in fear as the reports of destruction reach the outside. Devastating aftershocks will follow, with hundreds of tremors hitting almost daily for months.

Businesses will be wiped out. Churches will be destroyed. Schools will crumble. Amusement parks will be shattered. The dead will be everywhere. In some areas, only rescue helicopters will be able to get in with help. It will be far worse than the destruction of Nicaragua. All communications will be hampered. The wheels of society will come suddenly to a halt. All this destruction, death, and terror will happen in less than two minutes of divine judgment.

A series of minor earthquakes will precede the major killer quakes. One of moderate magnitude will strike, with moderate damage, and many will be relieved that a massive quake did not happen. But it will follow, most assuredly.

> . . . and the earth shall shake at my presence . . .
> (Ezekiel 38:20 KJV)

Judgment Begins on the Coasts

God's judgments have always begun at the "entrance gates" of nations, cities, and empires: "A cry of alarm will begin at the farthest gate. . . ." (Zephaniah 1:10 LB).

This is representative of the seaports, harbors, and centers of influx. It is significant that most of the Old Testament prophets warned of judgment beginning at the coasts. Zephaniah warned the Philistine cities: ". . . woe to you . . . living on the coast. . . . The Lord will destroy you. . . . The coastland will become a pasture . . ." (Zephaniah 2:5,6 LB).

Jeremiah, another prophet, warned nations that God's judgments begin as whirlwinds on the coasts of their lands, then spreading from one end to the other:

> Thus saith the Lord of hosts, Behold, evil shall go forth from nation to nation, and a great whirlwind shall be raised up from the coasts of the earth.
> (Jeremiah 25:32 KJV)

The West Coast of this nation has already been forewarned by scientists of an impending earthquake disaster. San Francisco is the dirt capital of America. It is becoming the homosexual haven of the whole world. Millions living in southern California are addicted to ease, eating, wining, dining, and prosperity. There are thousands of God-fearing Christians who refuse to partake of their sins, but many of them are not expecting judgment. Even Christians are turning a deaf ear to these warnings. They will be rudely awakened in a moment of time.

> Because sentence against an evil work is not executed speedily, therefore the heart of the sons of men is fully set in them to do evil.
>
> (Ecclesiastes 8:11 KJV)

Scientists Will Debunk Judgment Theory

The coming earthquakes will not be attributed to God's judgment on America. Instead commentators, government leaders, scientists, and other "experts" will try to explain it all as expected natural disasters. They will say, "We knew it was coming. We warned cities to prepare. We know how it happened. The underground shelves moved and earthquakes were triggered."

They are unwilling to admit that God controls each "natural" movement, manipulates every fault, and determines the exact minute and magnitude of every disaster.

And how do we know God plans and pinpoints all earthquakes? Because Jesus Christ warned of great earthquakes and famines coming to the last generation.

God warned Israel of a terrible earthquake two years before it happened. Amos, a sheepherder, was sent "two years before the earthquake" (Amos 1:1 KJV).

This prophet heard God's subterranean thunder and warned his nation that God was about to rise up and roar in judgment. He warned the earthquake was inevitable, with God saying, "I will not turn away the punishment thereof . . ." (Amos 1:3 KJV).

This humble prophet summed up his warnings by

saying, "When God is through waiting, he starts wasting."

Earthquake Humor

America sits on a powder keg of massive earthquakes—and jokes about it. Doom humor is now popular all over the nation. Men laugh and scoff at the warnings of coming disasters. And when small earthquakes strike as warnings of what will come, the quake jokes and sick disaster mirth begin.

I was in a small earthquake near Memphis, Tennessee, recently. I was on the eleventh floor of a hotel that began to sway. It was a scary experience. The following day, the front page of the Memphis *Commercial Appeal* carried a series of "quake jokes." It angered me. That quake could have killed many people. The paper should have carried a headline banner screaming, "Thank God for mercy!" Instead we insult God's warnings with barbarous scorn. Shame on us!

One day soon all the jokes will die out. All the laughter will vanish. And our nation will weep. Thousands will lie buried in heaps of rubble. The laughter and scorn will boomerang on the wicked.

God has made the sins of evil men to boomerang upon them! He will destroy them by their own plans. Jehovah our God will cut them off.
(Psalms 94:23 LB)

The Survivors

Many will survive. Among the survivors will be those who were prepared and who had humbled themselves before God. Those who heard the warnings and who began to trust God for deliverance will survive. Many unconcerned Christians will be lost, along with the thousands of unbelievers. They will be saved as by fire.

They will be saved through the destruction of their flesh. Delivered by death.

Out of the rubble will come a praising remnant. They will be led out to safety. Should Christ's coming be delayed it will be years before there will be even a partial resemblance of the former days. Those who remain will be terrorized by great aftershocks and hundreds of tremors. Those evacuated and those who eventually escape the epicenter will be fearful of ever returning.

Hundreds of God's children walked out of the ruins of horrible earthquakes in Nicaragua, Guatemala, Alaska, and elsewhere. And God will lead a host of the redeemed out of the rubble left by the earthquakes coming to this nation.

> Though a thousand fall at my side, though ten thousand are dying around me, the evil will not touch me. I will see how the wicked are punished but I will not share it.
>
> (Psalms 91:7,8 LB)

> . . . he has chosen some to survive.
>
> (Joel 2:32 LB)

2. Droughts

> When I shall send upon them the evil arrows of famine, which shall be for their destruction, and which I will send to destroy you: and I will increase the famine upon you, and will break your staff of bread. . . .
>
> (Ezekiel 5:16 KJV)

A second judgment zone will be stricken with drought. Long, tragic drought. Rivers and streams will dry up. Water tables will no longer support irrigation systems. Crops will wither and die in the fields. Winds will carry away topsoil, and this nation will suffer its worst dust bowl in all its history. None has been like it before, and none will ever be like it again.

The drought will spread and cover thousands of square miles. Smaller dry zones in various parts of the nation will also develop. Thousands of acres are already in dust-bowl condition.

Runaway Food Prices

The threat of major food shortages in the United States will cause a wave of hoarding. Stockpiling of food staples will lead in turn to runaway inflation of food prices. Flour, dried foods, sugar, rice, beans, and canned foods will skyrocket in price. Supermarket shelves will be emptied of staple items. A wave of fear buying will cause shortages in other markets. The masses who were purchasing high-priced items will go wild trying to stockpile bare essentials.

Alas, this terrible day of punishment is on the way. Destruction from the Almighty is almost here! Our food will disappear before our eyes; all joy and gladness will be ended in the Temple of our God.

(Joel 1:15,16 LB)

Killer Instincts for Survival

A tidal wave of fear always strikes when the populace begins to realize the dire consequences a drought-stricken nation faces. Animal instincts of survival surface and guns and ammunition sell at a record pace. The price of dried foods will eventually more than quadruple. People will be prepared to kill in defense of their hoarded food supplies.

Drought will, at the same time, be spreading throughout provinces of China and Russia. Russia will be faced with near-famine conditions and will try to rape Canadian and Australian wheat crops. The United States will eventually be forced to reduce all foreign sale of grains.

Shortages at home and a loss of all national stockpiles will trigger the wave of private stockpiling by individual homeowners.

Sons of dust, when the people of this land sin against me, then I will crush them with my fist and break off their food supply and send famine to destroy both man and beast.

(Ezekiel 14:13 LB)

No Secondary Causes

There is no such thing as an accidental failure of crops. There are no secondary causes. It is God who shuts off the supply of food. God holds the key to clouds. All the water supply is in His hand. He measures every drop of rain and sends it to its chosen destination.

Scientists will try to explain the drought as just another dry cycle. They see only secondary causes such as weather cycles, pollution, wind patterns. They refute the Bible that says, "It is God who turneth a fruitful field into barrenness for the wickedness of them that dwell therein . . ." (Psalms 107:33,34).

The same God who judged ancient Egypt by drought, who is even now judging other nations of this world with famine, will also judge America with severe drought: ". . . Thou art the land that is not cleansed, nor rained upon in the day of indignation" (Ezekiel 22:24 KJV).

Speak of blindness to judgment. Drought had burned up all the pastures of Israel. The trees and vineyards were all destroyed. Lakes, streams, and springs were dry as dust. Water was being sold at high prices. Yet Israel would not admit it was divine judgment.

. . . Israel doth not know, my people doth not consider.

(Isaiah 1:3 KJV)

God's most used, most powerful, most feared instrument of judgment has been, and always will be, drought and famine—the destruction of crops, the halting of harvest.

Judgment is the taking away of the means by which evil men gratify their lusts and appetites. God promised Noah He would never again destroy the earth with an overflowing flood, and that "seed time and harvest time" would remain intact. Yet, years later, deadly arrows of famine fell in various societies when sin was being judged. There will never be a total suspension of food growing and harvesting. God must feed His children. But that does not hinder God from judging nations by halting and hindering food production in various breadbasket areas.

One-fourth of the population of Ireland died in 1847 with the loss of just its potato crop. The potato famine devastated that nation, and all the wealth of England could not save Ireland. Drought and famine do more damage than an invading army.

"I sent you hunger," says the Lord, "but it did no good; you still would not return to me. I ruined your crops by holding back the rain three months before the harvest. I sent rain on one city, but not another. While rain fell on one field, another was dry and withered. People from two or three cities would make their weary journey for a drink of water to a city that had rain, but there wasn't ever enough. Yet you wouldn't return to me," says the Lord.

(Amos 4:6–8 LB)

The Corn, the Wheat, and the Meat

When God judges a nation with drought, the corn, wheat, and meat begin to be cut off. Joel, the prophet

73

quoted by Jesus and the disciples, warned this last generation of a horrible drought coming to the world. I believe America is included in this amazing prophecy:

The fields are bare of crops. Sorrow and sadness are everywhere. The grain, the grapes, the olive oil are gone. Well may you farmers stand so shocked and stricken; well may you vinedressers weep. Weep for the wheat and the barley too, for they are gone. The grapevines are dead; the fig trees are dying; the pomegranates wither; the apples shrivel on the trees; all joy has withered with them. O priests, robe yourselves in sackcloth. O ministers of my God, lie all night before the altar, weeping. For there are no more offerings of grain and wine for you. Announce a fast; call a solemn meeting. Gather the elders and all the people into the Temple of the Lord your God, and weep before him there. Alas, this terrible day of punishment is on the way. Destruction from the Almighty is almost here! Our food will disappear before our eyes; all joy and gladness will be ended in the Temple of our God. The seed rots in the ground; the barns and granaries are empty; the grain has dried up in the fields. The cattle groan with hunger; the herds stand perplexed for there is no pasture for them; the sheep bleat in misery. Lord, help us! For the heat has withered the pastures and burned up all the trees.

(Joel 1:10–19 LB)

Pestilence and Prayer Meetings

Scientists may try to explain the spreading drought conditions as another dry cycle, but they will not be able to explain away the infestation of worms and pestilences of crop- and root-destroying insects that are coming. Prayer meetings and days and weeks of prayer will not break this drought. God will not permit unrepentant men to escape judgment by simply mouthing meaningless calls for relief . . . "For the rains he sends are tokens of forgiveness" (Joel 2:23 LB).

Christian farmers will also be affected. Their land will wither and dry, along with their unconverted neighbors'. This drought will fall upon the just and the unjust. Everyone's lifestyle will be affected. But, the angel of the Lord will camp about those who fear Him, and God will lift the burden of suffering from the backs of the righteous. In the midst of the trial, God will appear as a righteous supplier of every essential need. Good times, easy-money times will vanish—but the true value of the Christ-life will flourish. In the end, God's children will survive and come forth having lost nothing of real importance and value.

> The sinners among my people shake with fear. "Which one of us," they cry, "can live here in the presence of this all-consuming, Everlasting Fire?" I will tell you who can live here: All who are honest and fair, who reject making profit by fraud, who hold back their hands from taking bribes, who refuse to listen to those who plot murder, who shut their eyes to all enticement to do wrong. Such as these shall dwell on high. The rocks of the mountains will be their fortress of safety; food will be supplied to them and they will have all the water they need.
>
> (Isaiah 33:14–16 LB)

3. Bankruptcies and Economic Chaos

". . . business has ground to a halt . . ." (Jeremiah 14:2 LB).

God will judge this nation with economic disasters. Critical money problems will strike large and small cities alike.

75

State and local governments will hang over the brink of bankruptcy.

> The rich man thinks of his wealth as an impregnable defense, a high wall of safety. What a dreamer!
>
> (Proverbs 18:11 LB)

The Fall of New York City

New York City faces economic and social disaster! The sword of judgment hanging over that city will fall suddenly. Overnight changes will happen—changes never before known to the American mind. *Bankruptcy will happen!* A temporary reprieve will falter. Short-range encouraging signs will be swallowed up in lightninglike events that will bring on bankruptcy. America's queen city will declare bankruptcy.

> Trust in your money and down you go! Trust in God and flourish as a tree!
>
> (Proverbs 11:28 LB)

> All your greedy businessmen, all your loan sharks—all will die.
>
> (Zephaniah 1:11 LB)

Shotgun Riders

Unpaid workers will take to the streets. Warehouses will be looted by angry mobs of workers. Trucks will be overturned in the streets. The produce markets will become places of violence and bloodshed Food suppliers will ride into the city with shotgun riders. A wave of union strikes will add to the confusion. Newark, New Jersey, and surrounding metropolitan areas will follow into bankruptcy. Police protection will become almost nonexistent. Instead, unemployed members of police associations will join in acts of violence and looting.

. . . for all the merchant people are cut down; all they that bear silver are cut off.

(Zephaniah 1:11 KJV)

Murder in Manhattan

There will be violence everywhere. Unheard-of violence. Unbelievable violence. Unnecessary violence. Uncontrollable violence. The violence that has been seething beneath the surface for years will explode. No city street will be safe. Teen gangs will once again erupt with unparalled waves of violence. The aftermath of it all is an outbreak of raping, murdering, and burning. God's judgment will not be recognized or accepted. Men will curse God, and a spirit of lust and greed will overtake millions. An Antichrist spirit will spread like terminal cancer.

And I will bring distress upon men, that they shall walk like blind men, because they have sinned against the Lord: and their blood shall be poured out as dust, and their flesh as the dung.

(Zephaniah 1:17 KJV)

Financial Fiascoes

The entire nation will tremble with economic and social upheaval. Investors who just weeks before boasted that no end of the good times was in sight will go scurrying like drowning rats to seek shelter from the economic storm. Pensioners will suffer the most. Food lines will appear once again. But, unlike the last depression, the long lines will not be docile. Anger, bitterness, and rebellion will be the order of the day.

Sales of Cadillacs, Mercedes, and other expensive cars will plummet. Furs, jewels, gold, silver, and other high-priced nonessentials will be nearly impossible to sell.

And so I have taken away these wondrous blessings from them. This sin has robbed them of all of these good things.

(Jeremiah 5:25 LB)

The fall of New York City will be but the first tolling of the bell of divine judgment. The ringing of that bell will be heard around the world. It will be a fearful sound. Experts will be astounded by the unexpected events that begin to unfold. No one could have accurately predicted the overlapping of events and tragedies. One bad report will lead to another. Judgment will come upon judgment. The rich will wail and weep. The poor will wander the streets, helpless.

> The nations rant and rave in anger—but when God speaks, the earth melts in submission and kingdoms totter into ruin.
>
> (Psalms 46:6 LB)

A Multinational Curse

Europe, Asia, and Russia will quake in fear at the news coming out of this judgment area. World money markets will go wild. Billions in the world currencies will be transferred from one nation to the other. Frantic currency manipulations will cause Arabs to threaten a boycott of world banking systems. Investment markets around the world will be thrown into a state of helpless bewilderment. Oil cartels, multinational corporations, and all others who tried to get rich quick will be cursed with economic confusion.

> An inheritance may be gotten hastily at the beginning; but the end thereof shall not be blessed.
> (Proverbs 20:21 KJV)

> They are swindlers and liars, from the least of them right to the top!
>
> (Jeremiah 6:13 LB)

The stock market will plunge again. The federal government will not be able to bail out the cities falling into bankruptcy. Fear will once again prevail over the American economy, one disaster will precipitate another. Drought will escalate food prices. This nation is headed for runaway inflation, and all the mental wizardry of our most brilliant experts will not be able to turn the tide. What worked before to take the steam out of inflation will this time only be fuel for the fire.

God clearly warns in the Bible that judgment zones are inflicted with high energy and fuel costs. When Israel was under punishment from God, the people cried, "We must even pay for water to drink; *our fuel is sold to us at the highest of prices*" (Lamentations 5:4 LB. *Italics added*).

> Your income disappears, as though you were putting it into pockets filled with holes!
>
> (Haggai 1:6 LB)

Rising Unemployment

What God did to the city of Jerusalem in the time of the prophet Zechariah, He will again do to the cities of America. When building the temple, the inhabitants were reminded what God did when judgment was upon them: ". . . there were no jobs, no wages, no security . . . crime was rampant" (Zechariah 8:10 LB).

The prophet Hosea gives a vivid description of what can happen overnight to a business boom. He said it vanishes like dew, blows away like chaff, and disappears like smoke:

> Therefore they shall be as the morning cloud, and as the early dew that passeth away, as the chaff that is driven with the whirlwind out of the floor, and as the smoke out of the chimney.
>
> (Hosea 13:3 KJV)

Gold may enjoy a temporary rise in value, but God's Word emphatically states that gold will be worthless in the day of His judgment. America, in its hour of judgment, has millions of people who hoard gold and silver. Coins, ingots, jewelry, all put away as a hedge against bad times. What a loss they will all suffer. Anyone who reads the Bible knows what happens to gold and silver when calamities strike.

Look at the record. Jerusalem is invaded by enemy armies, sent by God to judge the wicked. The city is in chaos and confusion:

> Those who used to eat fastidiously are begging in the streets for anything at all. Those brought up in palaces now scratch in garbage pits for food. For the sin of my people is greater than that of Sodom, where utter disaster struck in a moment without the hand of man.
>
> (Lamentations 4:5,6 LB)

During that time tenderhearted women became so crazed by hunger they cooked and ate their own children (Lamentations 4:10 LB).

And what kind of value did gold maintain? It was absolutely worthless! Gold-inlaid temple walls were stripped and scattered on the streets (Lamentations 4:1 LB).

The gold and silver bugs of America will one day see all their supplies lose their value, dollar by dollar, until worthless. Like sand seeping from a bag with holes in it.

> Your silver and gold will be of no use to you in that day of the Lord's wrath. You cannot ransom yourselves with it. For the whole land will be devoured by the fire of his jealousy.
>
> (Zephaniah 1:18 LB)

80

Then at last they will abandon their gold and
silver idols to the moles and bats. . . .

(Isaiah 2:20 LB)

Swiss Banking Scandal

I have been warning for three years that a banking
disaster will befall Switzerland. It is coming as surely as
night follows day. The unnumbered Swiss bank account,
the very epitome of security, will one day be totally insecure. There is coming a movement of vast sums of
currencies. Scandals will be uncovered. The very foundations of the Swiss banking system will be shaken. The
Swiss franc will suffer much as a result. Those who fat-
tened their Swiss bank accounts, hoping to live beyond
the reach of danger, are going to get hurt, badly. God's
word predicts it.

Woe to you for getting rich by evil means, attempting to live beyond the reach of danger.

(Habakkuk 2:9 LB)

6

The Unprepared Society

1. Good Times Ahead?

America is about to be chastised by divine judgment,
and its people are totally unprepared. Most won't believe "doom" preaching in such good times.

This book was finished in April of 1976, a bicentennial year. While I preach judgment, the false prophets of our government and economy preach "good times
ahead." I quote from *U.S. News and World Report*,

April 19, 1976: "Business forecasters predict a long spell of good times." The forecasters stated, "Worries are fading, optimism is spreading. The upward trend will continue, perhaps for years to come. The outlook is sparkling, and all sales and income are up. Economic pulse is beating stronger. A tremendous time for investment." (Reprinted by permission.)

This is my warning to my people, says the Lord of Hosts. Don't listen to these false prophets when they prophesy to you, filling you with futile hopes. They are making up everything they say. They do not speak for me! They keep saying to these rebels who despise me, "Don't worry! All is well"; and to those who live the way they want to, "The Lord has said you shall have peace!" But can you name even one of these prophets who lives close enough to God to hear what he is saying? Has even one of them cared enough to listen?

(Jeremiah 23:16–18 LB)

These kinds of false prophecies cause Americans to keep on ho-humming their way to hell. These smooth-tongued prophets of prosperity ridicule the doomsayers and preachers of judgment. They tell Americans, "All is well—no trouble or calamity is coming. Look about you; see all the good signs. Prosperity, peace, and plenty, because God is with us." These experts borrow their messages of prosperity from each other, all outdoing the others with predictions of a bullish market. They hope to talk the country into a boom.

So I stand against these "prophets" who get their messages from each other—these smooth-tongued prophets who say, "This message is from God!" Their made-up dreams are flippant lies that lead my people into sin. I did not send them and

they have no message at all for my people, says the
Lord.

(Jeremiah 23:30–32 LB)

2. Remember Lot

I see most American Christians as being just like Lot.
They live on the brink of disaster, totally unaware of its
coming.

Lot was a righteous man, according to the Bible. And
yet God did not warn him that his city of Sodom would
be wiped out. Jonah was warned about the destruction
of Nineveh. Noah was warned about the drowning of
his society. And Abraham was warned of the fire that
would fall and consume Sodom. Lot was not warned,
even though, like all the others, he was a righteous man.

Why didn't this good man know beforehand that his
society was in its midnight hour? Why didn't he go
about the streets preaching a warning like Jonah did in
Nineveh? Why didn't Lot leave Sodom like the children
of Israel left Egypt, with cattle, children, relatives and
family all saved and delivered? Why did he escape by
the skin of his teeth? Why was he so totally unprepared? This rich man barely escaped hours before the
disaster and ended up penniless, hungry, hiding in a cave.

Think of it! Abraham has already been warned and
is interceding with God for mercy on the city. Two angels approach the gate with a mandate from heaven to
destroy the city within twenty-four hours, if necessary.
And in this momentous time, what is God's man Lot
doing? Lot is sitting at the gate, nonchalantly slapping
friends on the back, climbing the social ladder, busily
making more friends and more money. He eats, drinks,
buys, sells, laughs, and plans with not one iota of discernment about coming judgment.

I see him sitting there at ease, prosperous and looking toward the future with confidence. And I want to go
up to him, lift him by the back of the neck, shake him,

and cry, "Wake up, Lot. Don't you know this fun, laughter, and prosperity are false? Don't you hear the warnings? Don't you know judgment is just around the corner? Are your spiritual eyes so dim, your ears so heavy you can't see or hear the trumpet call of God?"

Will Americans listen to preachers like me, who warn of judgment during good times? Well, hardly! Not any more than Lot's children listened to him. When Lot finally did get the message, he ran with great alarm to warn his family to prepare. Time was short; action and preparation were necessary immediately. They laughed. Just as people laugh at me for warning them of soon-to-come judgment.

> And Lot went out, and spake unto his sons in law, which married his daughters, and said, Up, get you out of this place; for the Lord will destroy this city. But he seemed as one that mocked unto his sons in law.
>
> (Genesis 19:14 KJV)

The church pews today are packed with people just like Lot. Good, sincere, God-fearing people who, like Lot, have vexed their minds so much that God cannot get His warnings through to them. "For that righteous man dwelling among them, in seeing and hearing, vexed his righteous soul from day to day with their unlawful deeds" (2 Peter 2:8 KJV).

3. The Mardi Gras Mentality

Societies headed for judgment turn to sports, frolic, drinking, and festivals. So it was just before the downfall of Rome, Nineveh, Tyre, Sodom, Jerusalem, and Babylon—all danced and drank through their last hours of judgment.

America is following the example of ancient Babylon. The empire was about to fall. The Medo-Persian army was only twenty-four hours away from a takeover of the kingdom. Over four million people were about to witness the swift judgment of Almighty God. Their king, Belshazzar, was victimized by a sense of false security.

It was the eve of judgment, and the city went wild. The festival held at the very hour of judgment was called SHACE, in honor of the goddess Shat. The entire city went on a wild, drunken binge. It was an adulterous carousal. Just like the American Mardi Gras with all its filth and provocation. "Belshazzar the king invited a thousand of his officers to a great feast where the wine flowed freely" (Daniel 5:1 LB).

God made one final attempt to warn these drunken people that the party was over. A strange and foreboding finger appeared in the great government banquet hall where the king and leaders of the nation were drinking from the sacred temple goblets. It wrote a message only Daniel the prophet could interpret. "This night, judgment!" was the content of the message.

Evidently the party continued, after the initial scare wore off. Back to the festival and fun. "Judgment? So what? We all have to die sometime. Live it up."

"That very night Belshazzar, the Chaldean king, was killed, and Darius the Mede entered the city and began to reign . . ." (Daniel 5:30,31 LB).

So it is in this, America's hour of judgment. A prosperous, ease-loving nation frolics its way toward the end. The epitaph God will place on our society is the same He placed on Noah's: "And they knew not until the flood came, and took them all away . . ." (Matthew 24:39 KJV).

4. Spiritual Wickedness in High Places

God help those men in high places who pretend to be righteous but whose fear of God is not according to truth. They claim to be children of the Most High God, yet they show themselves to be liars. They are ashamed of their God. They appease the wicked and exalt the haters of God. They call on God in public, but in the secret chambers of their hearts they fall before the idols of power and fame: "This people honoureth me with their lips, but their heart is far from me" (Mark 7:6 KJV).

They are not righteous, and they are not acceptable to God. Their lukewarmness is an abomination to the Lord. He will spew them out of His mouth. They sit as leaders of government, professing to be followers of the Son of God—but, in truth, are followers of their own lusts and interests. If they were truly the Lord's, they would lead the nation to repentance! If they were truly the children of God, they would resist the proud and wicked and would call for a return to righteousness. They would not be pursuing power by compromising their morals and ethics. They are nearly all power-corrupted.

Where are the nation's leaders who profess, "I am on the Lord's side!"? Where do they take their stand? Has the world heard their testimony? Are they satisfied to be secret believers? Will they bring a nation back to God through compromise and accommodation with wicked men? Will our President stand up and boldly declare his allegiance to his Lord at all costs? If not, God will begin now to judge the backsliding leaders of government! Their folly will bring upon them and their followers the complete wrath of God.

God has warned all government leaders of this land about what He will do to those who sell out to the idols of power and prestige! He brings the proud down. He humbles the mighty so that their memories are cast down in the mire. So will it be with all others who have begun in the Spirit but who now live in the flesh. Their counsel will bring them down in defeat and shame.

God's Word has some very sharp reminders for all government leaders, politicians, and candidates for office:

When there is moral rot within a nation, its government topples easily; but with honest, sensible leaders there is stability.

A wicked ruler will have wicked aides on his staff. When rulers are wicked, their people are too; but good men will live to see the tryant's downfall.

(Proverbs 28:2; 29:12,16 LB)

5. Three Reasons Why America Won't Listen

It is very difficult for America to accept a judgment message, for three reasons:

1 *Too Many Crackpots Preach Doom.* Sophisticated minds are so closed and cluttered, God cannot reach them with His warnings of judgment. Therefore, simple-minded people hear the Word and proclaim it. God chooses, even in judgment, to confound the wise by using the foolish things of this world:

But God hath chosen the foolish things of the world to confound the wise; and God hath chosen the weak things of the world to confound the things which are mighty; And base things of the world, and things which are despised, hath God chosen, yea, and things which are not, to bring to nought things that are: That no flesh should glory in his presence.

(1 Corinthians 1:27–29 KJV)

Perhaps that's why so many babes in thinking are warning of judgment. God will warn the nation, even if He has to raise up a motley army to do it.

One of the biggest laughs in New York City has to do with the judgment warnings of two little elderly ladies. Each week, for years, they have been chauffeur-driven in their Rolls Royce to Times Square. The chauffeur parks the limousine, opens the trunk, and hands each lady a sign. One reads, "The end of the world is near," the other, "Get ready." They parade up and down Times Square for an hour or two, then return to their suburban home. Multitudes laugh. It's a funny scene.

An old man parades in a sandwich sign, hand painted, with warnings about the end of the world. He passes out hand-scribbled tracts smudged with jelly and peanut butter. You can hardly read the warning— "Judgment is coming! Are you prepared?" People laugh.

Almost daily, I meet self-proclaimed prophets who go about telling their strange dreams, visions, and prophecies. Much of it is sad and silly. These misdirected people have turned off multitudes who now discount all judgment warnings as "fanatical." They cannot believe that a judgment message is compatible with the love of God.

> The time of Israel's punishment has come; the day of recompense is almost here and soon Israel will know it all too well. "The Prophets are crazy"; "The inspired men are mad." Yes, so they mock, for the nation is weighted with sin, and shows only hatred for those who love God.
>
> (Hosea 9:7 LB)

2 *Young Americans Have Never Known Hardships.* Most young Americans cannot even remotely relate to a judgment message. They have experienced so little of suffering and hardship. No food shortages, no lack of comfort or clothes. Parents have provided security and a whole catalog of material goodies. No wonder they can't imagine hard times coming.

Recently, a group of teenagers were surveyed and asked the question, "Do you believe hard times or depression is coming to America?" Ninety percent answered, "No, the government will bail us out."

A group of grandparents over sixty-five were asked the same question. The majority answered, "Yes. Hard times are coming again." The older generation had suffered and understood how it could happen again.

The social-climbing young married couples of America are angered by my warnings of judgment. They see judgment as a threat to their good times.

> But who will listen when I warn them? Their ears are closed and they refuse to hear. The word of God has angered them; they don't want it at all.
> (Jeremiah 6:10 LB)

3 *Americans Believe This Is God's Favorite Nation—Immune From Judgment.* This nation has been spared judgment and calamity. No foreign troops on American soil. No bombs. No severe drought or famine, as yet. And, in comparison with the suffering worldwide, even the Great Depression was not fatal.

Americans inwardly believe this is God's chosen nation. And He will never judge us, because we have defended the Jewish nation of Israel. God did promise to bless those nations that blessed the Jew. And He has kept that promise to America. But that does not make us immune from judgment. The same God who judged the sins of the Jews will judge the sins of gentiles.

Earthquake hits Nicaragua, and Americans rush to the rescue. We send boat loads and plane loads of clothes, food, and medical supplies. We bleed for the suffering masses there.

Earthquake strikes Guatemala, and the charitable process begins all over again. America mobilizes to help. Portable army hospitals, volunteers, funds for rebuilding. We feel sorry for those suffering friends.

Famine devours the starving masses in Biafra, Pakistan, and India. We send them tons of grain. Our students skip meals in sympathy. We grieve for the children who die hungry and swollen.

Then we think of America. "It can't happen here. This is a special place. Earthquakes, drought, chaos—

these things only happen elsewhere." We convince ourselves that America is an island fortress that sits like a queen of the globe, pretty, safe, and comfortable.

She has lived in luxury and pleasure—match it now with torments and with sorrows. She boasts, "I am queen upon my throne. I am no helpless widow. I will not experience sorrow."

(Revelation 18:7 LB)

This nation can't even conceive itself being a second-rate world power, much less a nation broken and wounded by divine judgment. It is one thing to be patriotic and loyal to our country. It is quite something else to shut our eyes to what has become of us.

It all boils down to three simple American delusions:

1. "End-of-the-world doomsday preachers are fanatical freaks."
2. "We've always come through every crisis and always will."
3. "America is too strong and resilient, and we are a nation of destiny."

This will be their line of argument: "So Jesus promised to come back, did he? Then where is he? He'll never come! Why, as far back as anyone can remember everything has remained exactly as it was since the first day of creation."

(2 Peter 3:4 LB)

7

The Unrepentant Society

Therefore also now, saith the Lord, turn ye even
to me with all your heart, and with fasting, and
with weeping, and with mourning: And rend your
heart, and not your garments, and turn unto the
Lord your God: for he is gracious and merciful,
slow to anger, and of great kindness, and repenteth
him of the evil. Who knoweth if he will return and
repent, and leave a blessing behind him; even a
meat offering and a drink offering unto the Lord
your God?

(Joel 2:12–14 KJV)

Will America repent? Will God spare us if we do?
What does it take to abort God's set judgments? Nineveh repented and was spared. Sodom was destroyed.

We have many Christians in America who believe a
great spiritual awakening is coming and that our nation
will turn back to God. That is the desire of God's heart.

America has already been visited in a mighty way by
God's Holy Spririt. We have witnessed a charismatic renewal, a genuine Jesus Movement among youth, and a
growing spiritual hunger among thousands of Christians. Yet, the wicked around us continue in their evil
ways. In spite of total saturation in the media of good
gospel preaching, in spite of the best religious freedom
in all the world, America has rejected Christ. Though a
remnant now turns to Christ, the masses go on unheeding
the call. Immorality marches on unchecked.

91

1. Redemption Through Judgment

The law of human history is that God's judgment is a necessary part of redemption. It is God's recovery plan for fallen nature. It is His way of weaning men from their sins. How can mankind ever be restored to God? When His threats are ignored, His mercy flaunted, His promises rejected—judgment is inevitable.

God always purifies through persecution. Judgment purges the wounds of society of poison and inoculates for the infections. God starves sinners so they would begin to hunger after Him. He makes men run in terror, hoping they will run right into His open arms.

Judgment is God grinding men down to size. He does not judge men only to appease the righteous indignation of some Christinas who yearn to see retribution. While the Christian hopes to see judgment against sin right now, God said, "My long-suffering endures to all generations." God is disciplined in judgment.

Your fathers would not listen to this message. They turned stubbornly away and put their fingers in their ears to keep from hearing me. They hardened their hearts like flint, afraid to hear the words that God, the Lord of Hosts, commanded them—the laws he had revealed to them by his Spirit through the early prophets. That is why such great wrath came down on them from God. I called but they refused to listen, so when they cried to me, I turned away.

(Zechariah 7:11–13 LB)

2. Shall I Pray for America Now?

To those who pray that God will spare America from divine judgment, I say—God will most likely answer through judgment! He will save America through judgment and will "remove the stumbling blocks": "I will consume man and beast . . . and the stumblingblocks with the wicked; and I will cut off man from off the land, saith the Lord" (Zephaniah 1:3 KJV).

Judgments coming on the earth should only encourage the Christian to pray and believe all the more for a cleansing and purging of perversion and violence. God is not running some kind of house of correction. He gave us freedom of choice. America has chosen its course, and there is no safe sanctuary outside Him.

God will purge out of the land all the idol worshippers and lovers of violence. This is exactly why God judged Israel. The prophet Zephaniah preached that:

"I will crush Judah and Jerusalem with my fist [says the Lord], and destroy every remnant of those who worship Baal; I will put an end to their idolatrous priests, so that even the memory of them will disappear. They go up on their roofs and bow to the sun, moon and stars. They 'follow the Lord,' but worship Molech, too! I will destroy them. And I will destroy those who formerly worshiped the Lord, but now no longer do, and those who never loved him and never wanted to." Stand in silence in the presence of the Lord. For the awesome Day of his Judgment has come; he has prepared a great slaughter of his people and has chosen their executioners. "On that Day of Judgment I will punish the leaders and princes of Judah, and all others wearing heathen clothing. Yes, I will punish those who follow heathen customs and who rob and kill to fill their masters' homes with evil gain of violence and fraud."

(Zephaniah 1:4–9 LB)

. . . those who are wise will not try to interfere with the Lord in the dread day of your punishment.

(Amos 5:13 LB)

Every true Christian should pray earnestly for America. Pray for a cleansing! Pray for the overthrow of wickedness and violence! Pray for a spiritual awakening that will reach every segment of our society!

But never pray to be spared judgment just so certain "Christian business interests" can be protected. I am growing suspicious of some who pray that America will be spared judgment. Too many are trying to protect their own personal interests. They need boom times to keep afloat. They are personally afraid of judgment because they fear the loss of money, business, buildings, and even ministries. If a child of God has surrendered everything and is free from the bondage of materialism, there can be no fear of God's judgment. A few seem to be praying, "Lord, save America from judgment so I can have more time to be more successful." God sees through all our phony burdens and proclamations of concern, and He knows every selfish motive.

Others say, "God can't judge America now because it must remain financially strong so that Christians can evangelize the world before Christ returns." I have heard all the prophecies and sermons about the great prosperity coming along with a great spiritual awakening. But, I am responsible only to God's Word, to preach what I know to be historically and scripturally true. God will always support the work of evangelism, even in hard times. The truth is that in time of judgment, Christians have always done more to spread the Gospel. The coming judgment will do more to straighten out Christian values, do more in bringing about a spiritual urgency, do more to break the spirit of confusion, than anything else God could do for this last generation. So let every Christian pray that God will do what He knows is best.

I hate your show and pretence—your hypocrisy of "honoring" me with your religious feasts and solemn assemblies. Away with your hymns of

praise—they are mere noise to my ears. I will not
listen to your music, no matter how lovely it is.

(Amos 5:21,23 LB)

3. God Does Change His Mind

The truth is, there is clear proof in the Scriptures that
in the history of man, God has changed His mind in
answer to fervent prayer. But no change has ever been
effected without national repentance and humility.
Sadly, there is no evidence of America's repenting,
other than God's own people who believe judgment is
coming.

What does it take to save a society from judgment?
The answer is found at Nineveh. The repentance of that
society is one of the great events in history. It will take
the very same intense repentance and reform to save
America. All the praying and talking in the world will
not save our nation, unless it produces Nineveh-like repentance. In Nineveh:

They believed the message of God! A fast was proclaimed, and the entire society was awed by the fear of
God. It started a revolution of repentance. The masses
forsook their pursuit of pleasure. Violence and sensuality were dealt a stunning blow, and crime was punished
severely. The proud wept in sorrow, and all phony
forms of religion were swept away by a complete turning to God.

Who can tell if God will turn and repent, and
turn away from his fierce anger, that we perish
not?

(Jonah 3:9 KJV)

All of society was affected! The rich and poor, government and society leaders, the good and the bad—all
covered themselves with sackcloth in true sorrow for
sin. It was not just a "revival of fear" or a spiritual

awakening of a segment. No! It was a top-to-bottom, through-and-through, social and spiritual turnaround. Business was halted so that values could be adjusted. The entire population was in agony over sin and rebellion against God. The king wept. The cattle and all animals were covered with sackcloth. Days and weeks of prayer and repentance were called for by the official government. Lawmakers turned to God and cried out, "We are sorry. Save us from ourselves."

> Beg him to save you, all who are humble—all who have tried to obey. Walk humbly and do what is right; perhaps even yet the Lord will protect you from his wrath in that day of doom.
>
> (Zephaniah 2:3 LB)

They repented without a promise of mercy! They were not told anything about a reprieve. They repented on only a warning, hoping for mercy. They had no Christ, no cross, no offer of divine grace. No great and precious promises. No great outpouring of the Holy Spirit! Yet they repented. America has had all God can give in the way of mercy methods, yet we do not repent. Why such severe judgments on America? Because people who sin against greater privileges and mercies are judged for refusing greater light.

> The men of Nineveh shall rise up in the judgment with this generation, and shall condemn it: for they repented at the preaching of Jonah; and, behold, a greater than Jonah is here.
>
> (Luke 11:32 KJV)

Do you know of any national move in America that even slightly resembles Nineveh's move to God? I don't. Our President gives only lip service to any genuine call to repentance. It must begin in our White House, it must include our Congress, then all our State Houses, then our counties, then our churches, then our house, every one of us! Nothing less! God calls it "turning from evil."

> At what instant I shall speak concerning a nation, and concerning a kingdom, to pluck up, and to pull down, and to destroy it; If that nation, against whom I have pronounced, turn from their evil, I will repent of the evil that I thought to do unto them.

> (Jeremiah 18:7,8 KJV)

4. Ten Indictments Against America

People who pray for America should be praying about the indictments of God against past societies. These are the things that grieved the heart of God in past history, causing Him to judge nations. Here is the list I found:

1. Your shepherds are slumbering, with no word from the Lord.
2. Your leaders, rulers are corrupted by power.
3. There is ease, mirth, and wild music in the land.
4. People are going backward to idolatry.
5. The prophets are laughed at and unheeded.
6. God is being robbed, and people grow covetous.
7. Religious leaders dialogue with doctrines of the devil.
8. The masses refuse their day of visitation.
9. People seek to establish their own righteousness and forsake the righteousness of God by faith.
10. They heap to themselves teachers, having itching ears.

America is called a Christian nation. Yet, we have more input with less output than other generations. We are seminar soaked, convention crazed, tape traumatized, and book boggled. Still, few seem to come into the knowledge of the truth. We seek exhilaration instead

97

of humiliation. The sum total of sin now outweighs the good. God is saying to us, "Return, because you have fallen—take with you words, turn to the Lord and cry, 'Take away all our sins and receive us back.' Then I will heal your backsliding, I will love you freely and I will turn away my anger" (Hosea 14:1,2,4).

> When Ephraim spake trembling, he exalted himself in Israel; but when he offended in Baal, he died. And now they sin more and more, and have made them molten images of their silver, and idols according to their own understanding, all of it the work of the craftsmen: they say of them, Let the men that sacrifice kiss the calves. Therefore they shall be as the morning cloud, and as the early dew that passeth away, as the chaff that is driven with the whirlwind out of the floor, and as the smoke out of the chimney. Yet I am the Lord thy God from the land of Egypt, and thou shalt know no god but me: for there is no saviour beside me.
>
> Hosea 13:1–4 KJV

5. Zephaniah's Message to America

The prophet Zephaniah very clearly shows us what a nation must do to be spared divine judgment:

"Gather yourselves together." Let everybody get together with one voice of repentance and contrition. Those "not desired"—the prostitutes, addicts, prisoners—all must come. Backsliders must return. It is either national repentance or national overthrow. The prophet is saying, "Do you want to be spared? Then get yourselves together and repent."

> Gather together and pray, you shameless nation, while there still is time—before judgment begins, and your opportunity is blown away like chaff; before the fierce anger of the Lord falls and the terrible day of his wrath begins. Beg him to save you, all

who are humble—all who have tried to obey. Walk humbly and do what is right; perhaps even yet the Lord will protect you from his wrath in that day of doom.

(Zephaniah 2:1–3 LB)

"Turn to Righteousness and Meekness." Humble yourselves and turn to holy living. "Let all the wicked forsake their ways . . ." while God's white flag is still flying. Quit talking about a gusto for life and talk about how to quit quenching the Holy Spirit. You must return to righteousness, and it must exceed that of Pharisees. God's mercy and sparing of judgment depend on three great big ifs:

"*If* . . . my people shall humble themselves. . . ."
"*If* . . . ye seek me with all your heart. . . ."
"*If* . . . ye forsake your wickedness. . . ."

I thought, "Surely they will listen to me now—surely they will heed my warnings, so that I'll not need to strike again." But no; however much I punish them, they continue all their evil ways from dawn to dusk and dusk to dawn.

(Zephaniah 3:7 LB)

6. A Divine Foreboding

There is now in many true believer's heart a "divine foreboding," an inner sense that God will send judgment soon. If I had never heard a prophecy, if I were not aware of all the signs of the times, if I knew nothing of the historical record of judgments—I would still know that judgment is near because of this powerful Holy Ghost "foreboding" in the depths of my soul. "We have heard a rumour from the Lord . . ." (Obadiah 1 KJV).

Some people try to quench those inner warnings, but they rob themselves of tremendous truth. The days are coming soon when no one will be able to dispel that inner trumpet.

Along with the foreboding is "an ever increasing awareness" of God's delivering power. A revelation of coming judgments is simultaneously a revelation of coming deliverance. Faith in God's acts of judgment must correspond with faith in God's acts of deliverance: "Surely the Lord God will do nothing, but he revealeth his secret unto his servants the prophets" (Amos 3:7 KJV).

7. Special Plans for Believers

God enters into judgment with a society with special plans and preparations for the safety of all believers. Provisions for their safety are made before the first blow of judgment is struck.

God's people are so dear to Him, He will change the course of nature to save them. An array of calamities may fall on this nation, but God will make a way of escape as surely as He did for the Israelites at the Red Sea.

God will walk with His children through the fires of judgment. As sorrows increase for the sinners, joys will multiply for the righteous. We are about to "enter the cloud," but in the storm, God's people will rest securely. Those who have God's glory will be able to stand God's gloom. Christ in the heart is the cure for the curse on our land. Believers can predict their own deliverance. Judgment then becomes our compass, showing the way to eternal redemption.

For the Lord himself will be a wall of fire protecting them and all Jerusalem; he will be the glory of the city. The Lord of Glory has sent me against the nations that oppressed you, for he who harms you sticks his finger in Jehovah's eye!

(Zechariah 2:5,8 LB)

Thus saith the Lord of hosts: If thou wilt walk in my ways, and if thou wilt keep my charge, then thou shalt also judge my house, and shalt also keep my courts, and I will give thee places to walk among these that stand by.

(Zechariah 3:7 KJV)

When Prayer No Longer Helps

Therefore pray not thou for this people, neither lift up a cry or prayer for them: for I will not hear them in the time that they cry unto me for their trouble.

(Jeremiah 11:14 KJV)

God said He would never cut a tree down until first it was ". . . digged about." God, in patience, says, "Give it one more year . . . dung about it, fertilize it . . . maybe fruit will appear. . . ." But there is an end to God's patience, and the time comes when He says, "Cut it down . . . it just cumbers the ground . . . useless . . ." (Luke 13:6–9).

The Bible gives four "states of stubbornness" that a society reaches—and when it does, all the prayers in the universe will not help:

1. When a society's crimes and violence go beyond the reach of remedy.

For my people's wound is far too deep to heal. The Lord stands ready at Jerusalem's gates to punish her.

Micah 1:9 LB

2. When the deadline is crossed and judgments are "set."

Son of man, when the land sinneth against me by trespassing grievously, then will I stretch out

101

mine hand upon it, and will break the staff of the bread thereof, and will send famine upon it, and will cut off man and beast from it: Though these three men, Noah, Daniel, and Job, were in it, they should deliver but their own souls by their righteousness, saith the Lord God. Or if I bring a sword upon that land, and say, Sword, go through the land; so that I cut off man and beast from it: Though these three men were in it, as I live, saith the Lord God, they shall deliver neither sons nor daughters, but they only shall be delivered themselves.

(Ezekial 14:13,14,17,18 KJV)

3. When a nation willingly rejects a widespread call to repentance.

Because I have called, and ye refused; I have stretched out my hand, and no man regarded; But ye have set at nought all my counsel, and would none of my reproof: I also will laugh at your calamity; I will mock when your fear cometh; When your fear cometh as desolation, and your destruction cometh as a whirlwind; when distress and anguish cometh upon you. Then shall they call upon me, but I will not answer; they shall seek me early, but they shall not find me:

(Proverbs 1:24–28 KJV)

4. When God has exhausted all His resources of reform.

For if we sin wilfully after that we have received the knowledge of the truth, there remaineth no more sacrifice for sins, But a certain fearful looking for of judgment and fiery indignation, which shall devour the adversaries.

(Hebrews 10:26,27 KJV)

Think of all the exhausted resources of reform:

Prosperity. He blessed America, hoping the goodness of God would lead us to repentance.

Prophets. Billy Graham, and a host of lesser-known men of God. All warning of judgment. All crying, "Get your house in order."

Threatenings. The Depression in the 1930s was a small threat. Small quakes, tornadoes, and upheaval in nature. God is warning.

Outpourings. Thousands revived. A Jesus Movement. A day of visitation. The masses reject!

Removal of Supports. One by one, God has removed supports of our lifestyle. Trusted institutions are in disarray. Even leaders are no longer trusted. Yet the more supports God removes, the harder men's hearts grow.

Secular Warnings. Aleksandr Solzhenitsyn, Toffler, Pauling, Browne, Cousins, Valery Giscard d'Estaing, and an ever-growing list of nonreligious prophets—all warning of impending judgment. Yet society shakes it all off.

> The alarm has sounded—listen and fear! For I, the Lord, am sending disaster into your land. But always, first of all, I warn you through my prophets. This I now have done. The Lion has roared— tremble in fear. The Lord God has sounded your doom—I dare not refuse to proclaim it.
>
> (Amos 3:6–8 LB)

God has no other resources left. He has tried everything. Judgment is the only weapon left. America is sinning a sin which could be unto death. Soon, unless we repent praying for America will be like praying for the dead. "There is a sin unto death: I do not say that he shall pray for it" (1 John 5:16 KJV)

103

8

Getting Ready

1. Preparation by Revelation

Man cannot prepare himself to face the judgment and terror of the Lord. All his attempts to safeguard himself and his family from danger are in vain. The Holy Spirit has been sent from God to reveal how and when to take specific action. God not only prepares the timetable of tribulation and calamity, he also prepares a specific timetable of preparation designed only for true believers. Only the sanctified children of God will have the total inside knowledge of future events and what steps to take in preparing for all the coming crises: "But God hath revealed them unto us by his Spirit: for the Spirit searcheth all things, yea, the deep things of God" (1 Corinthians 2:10 KJV).

2. Advance Knowledge

God did not send the death angel through the land of Egypt until he first warned all the Israelites of His forthcoming action. They knew in advance. They were told how to prepare. Specific and minute directions were given to the last detail. The timing was perfect. While the heathen Egyptians slept, oblivious to the oncoming calamity, God's people were busily preparing. They knew exactly what was coming and just what to do in order to escape His wrath. Suddenly that death angel's shadow covered the land. It was too late to act. The firstborn children of Egyptians, by the thousands, died mysteriously. But in the homes of the trusting Israelites—not a single death. All was peace and quiet. The nation wept and mourned, suddenly caught up in a national crisis. But in that same sinful nation, an underground of believers had received inside information! They escaped—because that has always been God's plan: to deliver His own from the wrath prepared for unbelievers.

> At that time Jesus answered and said, I thank thee, O Father, Lord of heaven and earth, because thou hast hid these things from the wise and prudent, and hast revealed them unto babes.
>
> (Matthew 11:25 KJV)

3. Experts Confused

God has purposely confused the minds of brilliant men who claim to be reading the future. They are blind and helplessly bewildered. Those who trust in the godless advice and prophecies of economists, mystics, and astrologers will lose their faith, their money, and possibly their very lives. Their predictions are all a pack of lies, revealing nothing at all about future events. They echo only what God has already spoken by the mouth of His servants.

God laughs at their proclamations and delights in exposing their false messages. Those who try to warm themselves by the fires of astrologers and horoscopers will end up cold and naked. The wisdom of the world is folly, and the false prophets arising today have not seen a single ray of divine insight. No satanic prediction will be fulfilled or verified by God's action. No! God will turn their lies upon themselves, and will make them laughing stocks among men.

> Then tell them: You're getting the wrong impression. I will fill everyone living in this land with helpless bewilderment—from the king sitting on

David's throne, and the priests and the prophets right on down to all the people.

(Jeremiah 13:13 LB)

4. Phony Prophets

Flee from these false prophets. Heed not the clamoring voices from government and business. Believe not their promises or their projections. Trust not in economists and experts who spew forth messages they hope will become self-fulfilling. There is not one single living man or woman on earth, other than God's messengers, who can reveal what is coming and how to prepare. *Not one!* Only those who walk with God have any knowledge of the future events. God never touches the earth with judgment until He reveals to His prophets and servants what He plans to do. It is the glory of God to reveal these to His own through His Word.

Let these false prophets tell their dreams and let my true messengers faithfully proclaim my every word. There is a difference between chaff and wheat!

(Jeremiah 23:28 LB)

5. The Handwriting on the Wall

As it was in the days of Daniel, so shall it be in the last days. God determined to judge the drunken King Belshazzar, his corrupt government, and all heads of state who mocked religion. Drinking alcohol from the holy temple goblets, they toasted the god of materialism and success. Those glib, positive-thinking professionals had no knowledge at all that enemy armies were already massing outside their borders. Suddenly, God's hand appears and writes a message on the plaster of the wall. No one in that nation—no one in that government, no court-pampered priest—could read the message. It was all bewildering. King Belshazzar called in all the famous

106

astrologers and mystics in the empire. "Tell me," said he, "what it means—quickly!"

Suddenly, as they were drinking from these cups, they saw the fingers of a man's hand writing on the plaster of the wall opposite the lampstand. The king himself saw the fingers as they wrote. His face blanched with fear, and such terror gripped him that his knees knocked together and his legs gave way beneath him. "Bring the magicians and astrologers!" he screamed. "Bring the Chaldeans! Whoever reads that writing on the wall, and tells me what it means, will be dressed in purple robes of royal honor with a gold chain around his neck, and become the third ruler in the kingdom!" But when they came, none of them could understand the writing or tell him what it meant.

(Daniel 5:5-8 LB)

6. Jeane Dixon Is Phony

The Edgar Cayces, the Jeane Dixons, the horoscopers, the stargazers, the palm readers, the fortune-tellers of those days were all dumbfounded. They could not decipher this prophetic message, because it was the finger of God. They could not recognize God at work, and in no way could they speak on God's behalf. See them, like little lambs, listening to Daniel, the prophet of God, as he unravels the warning: "Your days are numbered. You are weighed in the balance and are found wanting. The kingdom is lost" (Daniel 5:27).

I will put an end to all witchcraft—there will be no more fortune-tellers to consult. . . .

(Micah 5:12 LB)

A fool knows all about the future and tells everyone in detail! But who can really know what is going to happen?

(Ecclesiastes 10:14 LB)

7. Who Is Right?

Whom can you believe about the future? Who speaks the truth? Who can be trusted with speaking the one true message of warning and hope? Only the servants of the Most High God who are filled with His glory and who are not afraid to announce His message of judgment. From thousands of God's servants and handmaidens a message comes forth clear and succinct, verified by the Holy Word and confirmed by the witness of the Spirit.

> I will climb my watchtower now, and wait to see what answer God will give to my complaint. And the Lord said to me, "Write my answer on a billboard, large and clear, so that anyone can read it at a glance and rush to tell the others. But these things I plan won't happen right away. Slowly, steadily, surely, the time approaches when the vision will be fulfilled. If it seems slow, do not despair, for these things will surely come to pass. Just be patient! They will not be overdue a single day!
>
> (Habakkuk 2:1–3 LB)

8. The First Step in Preparing

The first step in preparing for the future is to tune in to the right message. No child of God need accept a message or a prophecy that strikes only fear in the hearts of the Lord's chosen people. The loving Father will not allow those who trust Him to be badgered and beaten down by misdirected prophecies. The message of doom and destruction is not aimed at trusting saints of God. These terrible judgment messages that come through His Word and by revelation are meant for the children of darkness. God never condemns the righteous, only sinners. When God, by His servants and prophets, sends forth a message of alarm and calamity, trusting believers must never appropriate it to their lives. Those who do, and those who react, are condemned by hidden sin. They become bruised by the message because they are standing in the line of fire. These messages of coming calamity are like deadly arrows shooting forth into the camp of the enemy. If you get in the line of fire, the arrow will strike into the heart and cause bleeding. Get out of the line of fire! Get off the middle of the road. Run from the enemy's camp, and get back to the safe shelter of the true believer. The child of God, living in victory and overcoming with faith, will always be able to hear with joy the message of doom and tribulation. The more calamitous and lethal, the more he rejoices—because he knows each calamity is another open door into the redemption age.

> You can be very sure that the evil man will not go unpunished forever. And you can also be very sure that God will rescue the children of the godly.
> (Proverbs 11:21 LB)

9. Are You Afraid?

Are you afraid of the message you hear? Do you choose to shrug it off, hoping for brighter days? Will you discount the message by discounting the messenger? Have you already closed your ears, determined to block out any word of warning from any messenger of God? How foolish! If God be with the messenger—if God has spoken His word and delivered it through lips of clay—then let every sincere believer go to that same source in humility and contrition and ask the Father if these things be so! God will not give you a serpent if you ask for a fish. He will not give you a stone if you ask for bread. The God who speaks forth His trumpet-like warnings will confirm it fully to all who diligently seek the truth. He who chooses to speak through a few will confirm it to all. Try the spirits. Test every message by the Word of God. Accept no prophecy from a person who profits from his message. The truest test of all is so simple that a child can measure it. True prophecy predicts doom for the sinner and deliverance for the saints. Gloom to the children of this world, glory to the children of Heaven! So hear then, child of God: When you hear the warnings of God depicting destruction and calamity, thank Him that you have been counted worthy to escape, and stand back and see the salvation of the Lord in the day of wrath.

> Though a thousand fall at my side, though ten thousand are dying around me, the evil will not touch me. I will see how the wicked are punished but I will not share it.
>
> (Psalms 91:7,8 LB)

10. The Second Step

The next step in preparing is to straighten out your priorities. You must determine right now what really means the most to you and your family. If your automobiles, your home, your pension, or any other material thing is first in your life, no amount of preparation can preserve it. You keep things in Christ by giving them up. You win over materialism only when you cut off its power over you. You cannot fear losing what you are no longer attached to.

Our fears mirror our loves. The man who loves to eat often fears the shortage of food. The woman who is married to her home and furniture fears not being able to pay the mortgage. The high-living person, attached to the good life, fears the loss of his job and the wherewithal to keep it all together. "Set your affection on things above, not on things on the earth" (Colossians 3:2 KJV).

11. Subjugate Your Appetites

You cannot prepare for the coming hardships and deprivations ahead until you bring under subjection all runaway appetites. How can we honestly tell our hearts we want to be ready for the hard times that lie ahead when we run out at every impulse and buy anything our emotions covet? We continue to waste, to squander, to go on buying sprees, to amass unneeded merchandise: toys, gimmicks, clothes, and expensive hobbies.

We lavish too much affection and food on overstuffed dogs and cats, while millions starve—and we claim to care. We say we would like to be ready; we wait for someone to tell us what to do and how to do it—but we turn it off when sacrifice and self-denial are called for! God has not promised to keep us in T-bone steaks and Cadillacs. He has not promised to defend and protect jet-set lifestyles. He has not promised to help you maintain all the projects and payments you have prescribed for your little kingdom. No! A thousand times no! God has promised to supply our *needs*. That may eventually mean soybean burgers instead of hamburgers. That may lead to a drastic change in lifestyle. It most certainly means a return to simple, basic values.

Let your conversation be without covetousness; and be content with such things as ye have: for he hath said, I will never leave thee, nor forsake thee.
(Hebrews 13:5 KJV)

12. Settle for Less

Begin now to execute acts of sacrifice and self-denial. Yes, that goes contrary to all the success preaching we have all been fed in recent years. Those expensive years will vanish! True believers will now gladly settle for less, that they may give more. My God wants me to prosper and be in health, but He has cleansed my concept of true prosperity. I am truly prosperous only when I yield over to the Lord everything I do not really need to be fulfilled and happy. I look into the future and I see the most difficult days the world has ever witnessed. I see a world groping for just a little ray of hope. I see the un-

111

raveling of society and hordes of hungry children. Then I hear again the word *prosperity*. Suddenly I know our Christian values have been distorted. Does God really want me to be so full when so many are empty? So rich when so many have nothing? Would God challenge me to believe this so-called prosperity instead of challenging me to be content with such things as I have?

> Then said Jesus unto his disciples, If any man will come after me, let him deny himself, and take up his cross, and follow me.
>
> (Matthew 15:24 KJV)

13. Cut Loose From the Tyranny of "Things"

Let us stop all this glib talk about "getting ready" until we are prepared to take drastic steps in getting *free*. Look over your world and all you own or hope to own. Then—emphatically, carefully, thoughtfully—cut loose from it all. In your mind, watch it all go up in smoke. In your spiritual mind, picture it all in ashes— gone, destroyed, worthless. Then add up what you have left! A redeemed soul! A heart anchored in God's rest! Love and joy. The Word of God assuring sufficient food and raiment. Angels camping all around you to keep you from danger. The Holy Spirit comforting and guiding. A Bible bursting with spiritual food. A glorious storehouse filled with daily benefits. A hope of glory. A home in God's world. Eternal life. The expectation of a new world with no sorrow or pain. And best of all, the 24-hour-a-day presence of Jesus—all the way to the end of time!

These are the true values. This is true prosperity and health! This is what God desires for us! The Word of the Lord is clear: "Disengage yourself from the bondage of things. You are entering a period of terrible warfare, and you must not be encumbered. Bring your body and all its appetites under subjection. Having food and shelter and raiment, be content! Be no longer a slave to the sin of covetousness. Trim your lamps and your budgets. Sacrifice with joy, and give to those in need. And all those things such as you need shall be added unto you. . . ."

Love not the world, neither the things that are in the world. If any man love the world, the love of the Father is not in him.

(1 John 2:15 KJV)

14. God's People to Be Delivered

God is not angry with His beloved. He is angry with sinners who refuse to heed His message. Those who love Him and trust His Word will experience the supernatural rest, calm, and assurance bestowed as a gift by the Holy Spirit. Blessed are they who hear the sound of the trumpet and prepare. Blessed are they who fear not—for He has promised to keep us from the day of His wrath. The shadow of death will pass overhead. The stench of death will reach our nostrils. Destruction will be viewed on all sides. But it cannot destroy the body and soul of any who hide in the shadow of the Almighty.

For the Lord loves justice and fairness; he will never abandon his people. They will be kept safe forever; but all who love wickedness shall perish.

(Psalms 37:28 LB)

15. Protected

In the midst of violence, God gives rest! While the earth trembles, God's children go forth in faith, trusting His promises of deliverance. In all shortages, He will supply every true need. Those who look for Christ's appearing will never have to beg for bread. There is a promise of food for the hungry, peace for the troubled, protection from calamity, strength for any crisis, light in

113

the midst of all darkness, life in the time of dying, joy in a time of weeping, calm in the midst of turmoil, shelter from violence, immunity from all plagues, hosts of delivering angels, purity in a time of filthiness, an open storehouse in the hour of shortages, an immovable foundation rock when floods rage, a hiding place from every storm, and a clear voice of direction when all other voices become confused!

Promises! Promises! That is all. But that is everything! Faith will feed on these promises, and faith will overcome. Faith in God . . . faith in Christ . . . faith in His eternal Word: That is the path of deliverance!

There is joy in God's camp. His children will march on unafraid: evangelizing, preaching, singing, rejoicing, filled with the Spirit—taking the Gospel into all the world—aware of but oblivious to judgment!

> Now I say that each believer should confess his sins to God when he is aware of them, while there is time to be forgiven. Judgment will not touch him if he does.
>
> (Psalms 32:6 LB)

9

Prepare to Meet God

1. Don't Be Caught Unaware

I had a very strange thing happen to me recently. It happened in my bathroom while I was washing my face. Suddenly out of nowhere came a still small voice: *"Prepare to meet God."*

I started to argue with my own heart: "I am prepared. I'm looking for the coming of Jesus—I expect

Him at any moment. I'm His child and no one can pluck me out of His hand."

But the voice I heard would not be quieted. Again, *"Prepare*—prepare to meet God." I got on my knees and prayed, "Lord, what are You trying to say to me? What do You mean, *prepare?"*

God began to reveal some truths to me that I had never before seen. And He also made it very clear I should share this message.

There are a lot of Christians who are not prepared to meet God. They are not prepared for the coming of Christ or impending judgment. What I am saying is, there will be many who consider themselves Christians and are thought of by others as Christians, who will be *"caught unawares."*

> Watch out! Don't let my sudden coming catch you unawares; don't let me find you living in careless ease, carousing and drinking, and occupied with the problems of this life, like all the rest of the world.
>
> (Luke 21:34,35 LB)

> So stay awake and be prepared, for you do not know the date or moment of my return.
>
> Matthew 25:13 LB

To prepare means to get everything in order, to do everything within your power to get ready and stay ready. Let me share with you now what the Holy Spirit warned me to do to prepare to meet God.

2. Make Your Final Move—Now!

God has brought this world to its final hour—the hour of decision! "Multitudes, multitudes in the valley of decision: for the day of the Lord is near in the valley of decision" (Joel 3:14 KJV).

The Bible tells of a time when Joshua was commanded by God to call together all Israel for a final decision:

> Then Joshua summoned all the people of Israel to him at Shechem, along with their leaders—the elders, officers, and judges. So they came and presented themselves before God.
>
> (Joshua 24:1 LB)

The prophet of God challenged them to make their final move. And here are the exact words of God to these undecided people: ". . . if you are unwilling to obey the Lord, then decide today whom you will obey" (Joshua 24:15 LB).

Make your final move! God is fed up; He wants a final decision. Get in or get out—*now!*

Once again the Holy Spirit is calling God's people to make their final move. *We know the end is near*—and you and I have to make our move now as to what kind of person we are going to be in the last hours. You are going to become more worldly minded—or more Godly minded. You are going to buy and spend and waste more—or give and share and surrender more. You are going to draw nearer to God and He to you—or you are going to draw nearer to your friends and the world and they to you.

The final move is on everywhere—it is evident everywhere you look. I have heard it, and so have thousands of other Christians who want to prepare:

> Come, my people, enter into your chambers, shut the doors behind you; hide yourselves as it were for a little moment, until the Lord's wrath against the enemy has passed. For, behold, the Lord cometh out of his place to punish the inhabitants of the earth for their iniquity. The earth will no longer be a hiding place for violent men. The guilty will be found.
>
> (Isaiah 26:20,21)

This is God's message to all true Jesus people: Make your move now—shut all doors behind you; hide yourself in Him. Get into the place of safety and protection because the Lord is getting ready to punish sin and the sinner. God has had it! This is it—*move now!*

3. Believe God for the Impossible—Now!

If your loved ones are ever going to be saved, it's now or never. Time is running out! God has given us many exact promises that we and "all our house" may enter the ark of safety.

But too many of us today are not really concerned. We have given up. We have time to watch hours and hours of soap operas on TV—along with football games, comedy shows, and late night movies—but no time to enter the secret closet and intercede for loved ones headed for hell.

God—shake us and wake us! Help us to get a "burden." Help us to weep and pray—and then believe for the seemingly impossible. We can witness miracles before Christ returns: ". . . with God, nothing shall be impossible" (Luke 1:37 KJV).

4. Get Ready to Leave—Now!

Some accuse me of being too negative lately. I have seen coming calamities—of judgment and persecution—and I've written much about it. I have been asked by friends to ease up and preach more "hope and gladness."

But, friends—what could be more hopeful or joyful for true Christians than getting ready to leave? I'm rejoicing and happy because I'm packed and ready to leave.

Sure, I'm staying busy, occupying time until He comes. But now I know we are working on a deadline. My values have changed. I intend to stay chin-deep in ministry to social and spiritual needs. But I'm working now with a "temporary visa."

This is God's final message to all who are ready to leave:

- ". . . be not entangled with this world. . . ."
- "Love not the world, nor the things that are in the world."
- "Set your affection on things above, not on things below. . . ."
- ". . . beware of the sin of covetousness."

5. Learn How to Handle Bad News!

Bad news is now epidemic. We hear news daily of crises, calamities, and shocking mayhem—and we shrug our shoulders and sigh, "What's next? Now I've heard everything."

One hardly has to be reminded of all the bad news we've been subjected to in recent months—kidnappers, energy crisis, shortages, famine, skyrocketing prices, Watergate, economic confusion, uncontrollable crime, drug addiction, killer tornadoes, landslides, earthquakes, and moral landslide.

We must also face a barrage of bad news in our personal lives. A dear friend calls to request prayer—he has just been informed by his physician he has cancer in his kidneys. A minister friend is rushed to the hospital after a massive heart attack. A loved one dies suddenly. A Christian worker suffers a bashed skull at the hands of a street gang. A Christian brother faces bankruptcy and the loss of everything he has. Grandmother is stricken ill. A mother weeps over a teenage son recently jailed for drug abuse—she begs for your prayers. Two close friends file for divorce—and you cringe at the thought of all the deep hurt their children will suffer.

Like it or not, the bad news keeps coming on, and there is no way to escape it. The Bible says, "The good man does not escape all troubles—he has them too. But the Lord helps him in each and every one" (Psalms 34:19 LB).

God's Word refers to bad news as "evil tidings." And the proper way to handle bad news is clearly revealed. Hear the sure word of God:

> Blessed is the man that feareth the Lord, that delighteth greatly in his commandments. He shall not be afraid of *evil tidings:* his heart is fixed, trusting in the Lord. His heart is established, he shall not be afraid. . . .
>
> (Psalms 112:1,7,8 KJV)

Oh, the wisdom and knowledge of our all-knowing Father! God looked ahead to this very generation, and He knew very well His children would be harassed by a flood of bad news. He sent His own Son to warn us of a time of unbelievable sorrows, when bad news would herald the good news of His return and the end of the world. He warned us that men's hearts would "fail them for fear," watching those terrible "bad news" things happening to the world. And Christians must be wary in reacting to all this bad news.

6. "Fix" Your Heart

Those of us who fear the Lord and delight in his commandments have been instructed to fix our hearts and establish our confidence. God's direct promise to those who love and trust Him is—"He shall not be afraid of evil tidings . . ." (Psalms 112:7 KJV). That is a promise! And a promise from God can become operative *only by faith!* Your fixed heart must cry out, "God said it. I believe it. That settles it!"

Don't allow any kind of bad news to make you afraid. Our God is still on the throne, and "all things still work together for good to those who love God and are called according to His purpose" (Romans 8:28).

Don't ever try to "live beyond the reach of danger."

You cannot hide from bad news or from calamity. The Bible warns: "Woe to you for getting rich by evil means, attempting to live beyond the reach of danger" (Habakkuk 2:9 LB).

David the Psalmist faced bad news head-on with confidence in Almighty God. He said:

> How dare you tell me, "Flee to the mountains for safety," when I am trusting in the Lord? "Law and order have collapsed," we are told. "What can the righteous do but flee?" But the Lord is still in his holy temple; he still rules from heaven. He closely watches everything that happens here on earth.
>
> (Psalms 11:1,3,4 LB)

Wake up, Christians! Get your eyes off the bad news. Turn it all into rejoicing and praise—because God is still on His throne and He is watching every move from Heaven. And our Father still has everything under control. So what in the world are you afraid of?

7. Practice "Promise Thinking"

School yourself in God's promises of deliverance. Learn what He promises to do for all who trust and obey. Be not ignorant of the Word of hope. Faith cometh by the hearing of these words of deliverance. Fear will overcome the wicked because they go into judgment ignorant of God's truth. God's people must prepare to go into the hour of judgment saturated with truth, fully persuaded that what He has promised, He is able to perform. There is no way to prepare without being fully clothed with the Word of promise. Read the promises! Hide them in your heart! They will be your source of strength in the crisis. God will respond to your claim on His promises, but how can you claim any Word you have not heard? The promises are for you. They are for your family. They are given for your hope, your protection, your assurance. Think often now on His promises. Rid your mind of schemes, plans, fears, and personal dreams—and fill it with truth. This will set your mind and heart free—free to face the future judgments with confidence and great peace.

> Whereby are given unto us exceeding great and precious promises: that by these ye might be partakers of the divine nature, having escaped the corruption that is in the world through lust.
>
> (2 Peter 1:4 KJV)

8. Expect to Be Delivered

Exercise faith for deliverance from God's wrath. It is not contrary to God's Word to convince yourself that God has a promise of deliverance from all calamities for you and your family. Instead, His revealed Word is an eternal testimony of how He delivered all who trusted in Him throughout all past generations. Plan to be delivered. Plan, by faith, to ride out every storm in the shelter of His wings. While thousands around you may perish in judgment, you can survive on faith! All your puny preparations offer no guarantee against calamity. All the child of God has or needs is a contract against calamity. All the child of God has or needs is a contract of faith. That contract is binding—when it is sealed with faith!

> Oh, how great is your goodness to those who publicly declare that you will rescue them. For you have stored up great blessings for those who trust and reverence you.
>
> (Psalms 31:19 LB)

Begin now praying a prayer of faith for deliverance. Pray with confidence that God will cause His protecting angels to become your guards. Pray for His angelic hosts to encamp round about you as you go to and fro. Pray for His loving protection on your loved ones at home while you are separated from them. This is scriptural. It is in the perfect plan of God. God is moved by this kind of confidence, and He will confirm His word on this matter. It is according to His will to pray for the fulfillment of His promises. Pray that you will be accounted worthy to escape all the coming calamities. And we are made worthy through the completed work of Christ in us! So pray confidently in His worthiness!

But O my soul, don't be discouraged. Don't be upset. Expect God to act! For I know that I shall again have plenty of reason to praise him for all that he will do. He is my help! He is my God!

(Psalms 42:11 LB)

9. Conquer Your Fear of Death

Look death in the face and conquer its fear! The wicked will die in fear. Death will be the conqueror over all the wicked on the day of judgment. But the righteous must not fear to die! God has provided victory over that fear.

Forasmuch then as the children are partakers of flesh and blood, he also himself likewise took part of the same; that through death he might destroy him that had the power of death, that is, the devil; And deliver them who through fear of death were all their lifetime subject to bondage.

(Hebrews 2:14,15 KJV)

Satan has no more power to frighten God's people when they are finally delivered from the fear of dying.

Do you desire a place of complete freedom from fear? Fear of the future? Fear of calamity and judgment—even though you know it is God who performs it? Then shake loose from the bondage of the fear of death! Death for the child of God must now be considered the ultimate healing. The key to life and death is in our Lord's hand. We who trust the Lord must look into

122

the future, filled with calamities and judgments—earthquakes, famine, violence, chaos, insanity—and cry out in faith, "Live or die—I am the Lord's!"

> For whether we live, we live unto the Lord; and whether we die, we die unto the Lord: whether we live therefore, or die, we are the Lord's.
>
> (Romans 4:8 KJV)

Now, nothing can hurt you! Nothing can alarm you! Nothing can shake your mind or spirit! You have faced the last and most powerful enemy known to man, and you see that God has turned your enemy into a friend.

> So when this corruptible shall have put on incorruption, and this mortal shall have put on immortality, then shall be brought to pass the saying that is written, Death is swallowed up in victory. O death, where is thy sting? O grave, where is thy victory? The sting of death is sin; and the strength of sin is the law. But thanks be to God, which giveth us the victory through our Lord Jesus Christ.
>
> (1 Corinthians 15:54–57 KJV)

10. Do Not Look for a 'New Revelation'

Revelations, dreams, visions, horoscopes, ESP, predictions, prognostications—none can be trusted as *the truth!* Dreams and visions by true men and women of God can spotlight the truth and explain what is already revealed—but only God's Word contains the truth that sets man free to act. "To the law and to the testimony: if they speak not according to this word, it is because there is no light in them" (Isaiah 8:20 KJV).

No new revelation is needed! We need to diligently search God's Word and find the answer to all our problems and questions. I, for one, will never again make a move, invest, act, or do anything else without first consulting the answer book—God's Word. New doctrines, new revelations, new prophecies—are all pouring out of certain charismatic and prayer groups delving into mysticism. Many will be deceived unless the church returns to the one and only true prophecy—God's Word!

Christians who believe in horoscopes ought to have their spiritual heads examined. The Bible calls it all a pack of lies.

> Don't act like the people who make horoscopes and try to read their fate and future in the stars! Don't be frightened by predictions such as theirs, for it is all a pack of lies. Their ways are futile and foolish. They cut down a tree and carve an idol. . . .
> (Jeremiah 10:2,3 LB)

Transcendental meditation is Satan's short circuit of divine revelation. It is a cheap mental game that is played by people who no longer believe or trust God's holy Word.

> Is it such a fast that I have chosen? a day for a man to afflict his soul? is it to bow down his head as a bulrush, and to spread sackcloth and ashes under him? wilt thou call this a fast, and an acceptable day to the Lord?
>
> (Isaiah 58:5 KJV)

10

Practical Preparations

1. Do Not Hoard Gold or Silver

Hoarding of silver and gold will not help. Study your Bible and you discover that jewels, silver, and gold *all fail* in the hour of judgment.

Your *silver and gold* will be of no use to you in that day of the Lord's wrath. You cannot ransom yourselves with it. For the whole land will be devoured by the fire of his jealousy.

(Zephaniah 1:18 LB)

Make no provision to trust in silver or gold. God will not protect those who trust in it. Silver and gold will not be a shelter in the storm. It will lose its value. It will be cast into the streets as worthless. It is a curse, and a man will one day give away all his caches of gold and silver for bread and water.

The man who puts his confidence in gold or silver cannot put his confidence in God. It is not wise to hoard gold! It is not prudent! It is not acceptable to God. Never in all history has gold been of any value in the day of crisis or judgment. The true child of God must not rely on money, materialism, gold, silver, jewels, or investments.

Therefore, O my people, though you are such wicked rebels, come, return to God. I know the glorious day will come when every one of you will throw away his golden idols and silver images— which in your sinfulness you have made.

(Isaiah 31:6,7 LB)

Let those who own gold and silver, and those who hold investments, become totally detached from them. Lay them on the altar of God and be ready to lose it all when judgment comes. Houses, lands, investments— these are all acceptable to God. He, in His wisdom, will guide and protect all the interests of those who yield them over to God in their hearts, using these things but not trusting in them.

They shall cast their silver in the streets, and their gold shall be removed: their silver and their gold shall not be able to deliver them in the day of

125

the wrath of the Lord: they shall not satisfy their souls, neither fill their bowels: because it is the stumblingblock of their iniquity.

(Ezekiel 7:19 KJV)

2. Settle God's Account

Settle all accounts with God. Owe Him nothing. Those who have robbed God in tithes or offerings are cursed with a curse. They will be judged. But God has given a special promise of deliverance to all who give Him the portion He asks. "They have cut themselves off from my help by worshiping the idols that they made from their silver and gold" (Hosea 8:4 LB).

Have you held back on God? Your good intentions, your promises are no longer acceptable. You must act quickly! Balance your books with the Lord now! Your life depends on it! Those who brush this message aside will soon understand that the curse declared by the prophet Malachi is the full counsel and truth of Almighty God:

Will a man rob God? Yet ye have robbed me. But ye say, Wherein have we robbed thee? In tithes and offerings. Ye are cursed with a curse: for ye have robbed me, even this whole nation.

(Malachi 3:8,9 KJV)

3. Don't Run

Do not seek to run or hide from judgment! There are no safety zones! God alone is our safety. He will pour out judgment upon the cities, upon the countryside— north, south, east, and west! There is no place to run! There is no need to run. He is God, no matter where you live. He directs all His people to occupy time until He comes—right where they are. Do not move unless clearly directed by God. Be at peace where God has placed you. You are in no more danger where you live now than you would be if sheltered in concrete bunkers.

126

Many are being prompted to move out of cities. God is raising up many "depots of blessing." These are Holy Ghost centers of evangelism and small cities of refuge that will one day be mightily used by God to bless thousands. But the God who calls some to the countryside is also calling many to a new dedication to evangelize the city. God's faithful army of children who live and work in the city will be granted special grace and power. They will be spared and delivered with a high and mighty hand. Only the undeserving, coldhearted Christian will suffer the loss of all things. Some overcoming Christians will be taken in the hour of judgment, choosing to be with the Lord rather than to be delivered.

There will be violence in the smallest towns, as in the city. Where there is no drought, there will be economic disaster. So there is no reason to seek a change of address. You who believe will carry your safety with you. In God, you are safe right where you are.

God's message to those who live in the cities—who live in the areas of severe earthquake, drought, social unrest, violence—is simply this: "Having done all—stand still and see the salvation of the Lord."

4. Don't Be Deceived by Human Prophecies

There are four kinds of prophecy: historical, inspirational, human, and false. It is possible for many Christians to be deceived by human prophetic letters, messages, and warnings that suggest dates, times, and seasons of judgment. Be careful; try the spirits.

Jesus warned of prophecies about ". . . going to the wilderness . . . or some secret place . . . go not with them. . . ." Never listen to or be alarmed by prophecies that suggest you run, hide, escape from judgment on a specific date or a specific place. The call of all true prophecy is to repent—not hide or run. "A fool knows all about the future and tells everyone in detail!

127

But who can really know what is going to happen?"
(Ecclesiastes 10:14 LB).

The Bible makes it very clear that all the times and
seasons are in "the Father's hand. . . ." And Paul said
we have no need to be troubled by letters, dates, or misdirected prophecy:

> It is *not* for you to know the times or the
> seasons, which the Father hath put in his own
> power.
>
> (Acts 1:7 KJV)

> Be not soon shaken in mind, or be troubled
> . . . by word, nor by letter as from us, as that the
> day of Christ is at hand. Let no man deceive you
> by *any* means. . . .
>
> (2 Thessalonians 2:2,3 KJV)

5. Go to Sleep

". . . so he giveth his beloved sleep" (Psalms 127:2
KJV).

God gives sleep as a gift to His children as surely as
He gives food and protection. It is as firm a promise as
any in the Book. The re-creating sleep God gives is a
crown He places only on the heads of His beloved, not of
strangers.

No power on earth can give you honest sleep. Artifi-
cial sleep from pills and capsules is false and transitory.
The giving of true sleep is the domain of God only. It is
His gift to believers.

Rising early and sitting up late to have more time to
fret and worry is the grossest kind of sin against God.
Trusters are good sleepers. Without moving a finger,
they employ God on their behalf because they are
wholly convinced He will do what He has promised.
While we sleep, God draws on our inner confidence to
create solutions to our needs.

God's Word promises, "When thou liest down, thou

shalt not be afraid: yea, thou shalt lie down, and thy sleep shall be sweet" (Proverbs 3:24 KJV). With the world crumbling all around us, and all seeming so insecure, to lie down in Christ's love and go to sleep is one of the greatest of all gifts.

God doesn't just *send* sleep, He personally delivers this gift. It is His own hand that shuts the eyelids. We consecrate our pillows, and His loving voice whispers, "Sleep, my child. All is well. Let me take over from here. Let me watch while you rest."

6. Quit Worrying

Some people work all day and worry all night. We act like possessed guards who have laid up in our storehouses something so precious we dare not sleep, lest we somehow lose it. Grasping, envious, materialistic people cannot sleep well. Contentment is the Holy Ghost tranquilizer that leads to sound and godly sleep. Your bed is often a "think tank" where goodness or mischievousness is devised. Therefore, we must bring every thought into captivity to the obedience of Jesus Christ.

All God's true children are entitled to His promises to grant the gift of sleep. Don't question your divine right. Rid your mind of all vain thoughts first. They are the culprits that hinder the receiving of this gift. These thoughts of revenge, immorality, and hopelessness are like a pack of murdering thieves who break in only to rob us of peace of mind and godly sleep. Prayer provides wings to fly above all these maundering thoughts.

Sleep is a direct result of feeling safe. It comes from fully trusting that God is really holding us up. Why do we not trust God to keep us safe through every storm and calamity? Simply because we are not sure of His promises! We are not sure they are for us today: Unsure that we understand what they mean. Unsure we are interpreting them in the light of our own needs. Unsure we can make them work for us. Unsure about our wor-

129

thiness to receive them. So we often prefer to stay in the dark concerning all His precious promises. Then, when we don't get what we expected, we have an excuse: "I don't understand, I guess!"

Sleep comes when you convince yourself you have a powerful Friend who promises to use all His great power and resources to make you safe and secure. Imagine a friend so powerful that no wind blows without His command—no earthquake or flood strikes without His permission—no famine or drought occurs without His word of judgment—no world leader breathes an extra breath without His granting it—no demon possesses an ounce of human flesh without His knowledge—no sparrow falls to the ground without His counting it—no hair sprouts on any head without His numbering it—no life exists without His breathing it. That is our powerful Friend who promises to give us the gift of sleep!

Our believing time becomes God's working time. We start God working for us when we start trusting. And since good nights lead to good days, we must let Him be our bodyguard twenty-four hours each day.

God never sleeps. "He that keepeth thee will not slumber . . . he that keepeth Israel shall neither slumber nor sleep" (Psalms 121:2,3 KJV). He never tires, never wearies. Nor does the devil ever sleep. But God never lets Satan out of His sight. God stands watch over His own. No intruder can take us unaware. He is "thy keeper." That is very personal. He is *yours*—all the time. Neither daylight nor moonlight calamities can overtake us. "The sun shall not smite thee by day, nor the moon by night" (*Ibid*, v. 6). And if God is protecting you, Satan can't have you—no matter how hard he tries. Who has all power? Who conquered death, hell, and the grave? Who made the devil His footstool? God! And a never-sleeping God will cause me to "lie down in peace, feeling safe, preserved from all evil!"

7. Practice "Pillow Faith"

God is better than bolts and bars. When you crawl up in God's bosom, learn to give up the guardianship of yourself. You can't sleep till you first "lay down." Lay down your problems, your illness, your anxieties. Leave tomorrow with God—He is big enough to handle it. A resigned will comes from knowing in whose hand you are.

Do you remember the child's prayer that goes "If I should die before I wake, I pray the Lord my soul to take . . ."?

The secret to lying down and sleeping well is to commit yourself into His hands as if facing death. Actually, if you are ready to die, you are ready to sleep. If He is able to see you through eternity, isn't He able to see you through tomorrow? God gives us "pillow faith"—that is, resting in God and trusting that in the night He will instruct us and allow us to awaken with a true sense of direction. "My reins also instruct me in the night seasons" (Psalms 16:7 KJV).

Hope is the Christian's security blanket. Wrap yourself in hope, and the cold blast of anxiety cannot chill your rest. Trusting God is simply shifting our burden.

Sleep of the godly is not incidental with God. With one hand He delivers mighty arrows of famine to destroy a sinful nation; with the other He lovingly delivers the gift of sleep to one of His children. You say God cannot be troubled with such trivia? Then you do not believe His Word! Not only does He deliver the gift of sleep, He lingers to count every hair on our heads. Cannot the creator of sleep, the inventor of rest, give it to those who ask in faith? And, if you can't count sheep, talk to the Shepherd.

In the midst of storms, thunder, earthquakes, drought, war, and violence, the trusting person can sleep unperturbed and serene in his confidence in God. When hard times come, faith will not shrink—because

He has promised to deliver us three ways: "our soul from death, our eyes from tears, our feet from falling" (Psalms 116:8).

8. Get Back to Simplicity

We need to go to bed uncomplicated. The Word says God preserveth the simple. Not the feebleminded, but those who trust God without complications. God delights in giving rest to simple people who, with pure minds, look only to Him for help and deliverance. Go to bed as a "God fool" who believes Him before all others as a way of escape.

God wants us to be comfortable with Him. Never nervous, uptight—but relaxed and confident in His presence. He wants to become so personally involved in working for us that we will lean on Him during all crosses and losses. Our God practices "divine discrimination"—that is, He is prejudiced in our favor. "Thy blessing is upon thy people" (Psalms 3:8 KJV). That should cause any believer to sleep in peace!

God is on duty at all hours—so lie down and claim His great gift of sleep. It's yours! Ask, and you shall receive.

11

Protected in Judgment

1. God Protects Me

The Psalmist cried, ". . . Thou art my God" (Psalms 31:14 KJV).

You will always be afraid of judgment until you can truthfully say, "God is mine—He protects me!" We must be obsessed with this truth, or there can be no certainty to our faith. This must be the one great fixed principle of our lives. He is mine, and I am under His personal contract of protection.

I must remember God is not fighting against me. He is *for* me! He wants my soul to prosper and be in health. He puts a lump of sugar in every cup of bitterness. And if He puts us out in a storm, He makes sure we have a good boat under us.

God is not only at work saving and convicting the whole world, He is busy working at saving just me. We never doubt His presence and power in the universe, but we doubt His presence and power in our own lives. We believe He cares for the needy, the down-and-outer, the addict, the prostitute, the hopeless—but we cannot seem to believe He is just as interested in us. God is not just "up there" engaged in running the universe—He is "down here" at work running my personal affairs. He is never so preoccupied with world affairs that He cannot hear the slightest whisper of my needs. He fills all the heavens, but He also fills my heart.

Here is where we corrupt our faith. We have a deformed, accommodating vision of God. We understand so little of Him; He appears as a blank, and our imagination paints in the image. Our thoughts are not His thoughts, and our ways are not His ways. His ways are as far above ours as the heavens are above the earth. But the danger lies in seeing God as one so big, so preoccupied with running the universe, that He cannot be interested in the small, personal details of our lives.

That is blasphemy. You make God what He really wants to be in your vision when you trust Him to be involved in every breath you breathe and every move you make.

2. God Alone Will Save

God is jealous and will allow no co-rivals for our deliverance. And there is not one intelligent reason why

133

God's people should fear in troubled times. If God be in us, He is as near to our problems as we are. If we were to fail or fall, He would have to fail or fall with us. If Satan sends his demon dogs to nip at our heels, he must deal with God—not us! When Satan knocks, we need simply answer, "Wait! I'll call the Man of the house."

It is not that we own God, but that God owns us. He is ours because He made us His. *My* God! Who dares say it? All who trust Him as the answer to everything. Then, when you have God's glory, you can rejoice in God's doom. You and I may live to see the wreck of matter and the crash of worlds—nevertheless, we will not fear. We will not fear noise, or force, or melting elements, shaking mountains, raging seas, withered fields—because our God sitteth King of the flood. The Alps and the Andes may tremble, but God's people will stand firm in faith.

3. By Faith Alone

Those who trust that God is protecting them are "agents of the possible." Faith is a window with a view of God; therefore, people who trust can never be guilty of "underliving." As agents of the possible, we must learn more and more how to live by faith. Think of it: "The just shall live by faith" (Romans 1:17 et al. KJV)—eat, drink, be clothed, be protected, be delivered *by faith.* How shall we live when depression and anarchy explode on us? By faith! How shall we live when shortages and violence threaten? By faith! How shall we live when unemployment, deprivation, and hunger surround us? By faith. We who have been saved by faith—who hope to be redeemed by faith—shall live and survive by faith.

No matter how black conditions look, "the earth is still full of the goodness of the Lord" (Psalms 33:5 KJV). God is still employed feeding a brimming ocean of fish. He still provides earth's creatures with food. Even ungodly men enjoy His sunshine and drink His refreshing water and breathe His life-giving air.

Prayer is the sum total of our power with God. God is employed through the prayer of faith. Prayer still opens the windows of Heaven, still moves the sun, still holds back the plague, tumbles stone walls, divides the sea, opens prison doors, shakes houses, and raises the dead.

It always seemed strange to me that some people believe the moon controls the ocean tides and that the stars control man's destiny—but they can't believe God controls anything. True Christians use faith to extract the goodness of God and to determine all future directions. Faith invites the pencil of the Holy Spirit to write all God's promises indelibly on the heart that they never be taken for granted or forgotten.

4. Total Security

One of God's greatest promises is security. But God gives not only security but liberty. He allows us to go forth in safety. We carry our security around with us. We don't go away to safety, as if to hide. We go forth *in* it. In the middle of all trouble and calamity, we walk in liberty. We are as safe in all the fires of trial as the three Hebrew children were. They went forth, in safety, into the furnace. Thank God for security—anytime, anywhere!

It appears at times that God is not working for us and that He stands calmly by without sympathizing with our trouble. But God's Word says He is "a very present help in time of trouble" (Psalms 46:1). He is a right now, right here, God! If we can know such great promises, we can intelligently claim them. That is not blind faith or devout ignorance. No—instead we can shout, with deep knowledge, "I know whom I have believed, and I am persuaded. . . ."

The worst fear in all the world is to think God is no

longer helping—that He is no longer protecting you. What is needed to counteract that fear is a transfusion of confidence that comes from hearing and believing the Word of God. Joyful Christians are the most believing, the most receiving, the most hopeful of all. We are too often so terrified by the feelings of the wrath and judgment of God that we cannot enjoy the laughter and joy of being safe in Jesus. The fact is, the joy of the Lord is our strength. If you have no joy in this troubled time, you have no strength to face it.

Trusting God to deliver you is just sanctified common sense. The result of faith is its best argument. Blessings and answers come not just to a few who trust, but to all who trust! To trust is to "sit like a mountain"—strong and immovable, awaiting the salvation of the Lord. It's a good way of living and a better way of dying.

I know God has set boundaries on all the suffering and troubles of His children. He will never allow His own to be pushed or harassed to an unbearable extreme. God will deliver us from the hour of tribulation—but subject to Holy Ghost timing. We are often afflicted with what I call "the sin of suddenness." We want God to work for us according to our schedule, even if we are not ripe to receive. Deliverance from hunger, from fear, from calamity, from violence—from all evil—is sure. But don't spend time figuring out how God will work it out. That is all in His hand.

God is employed! He delivers me! Why not let Him finish His delivering work in all of us?

5. Stormproof

If society is breaking down and the economy is falling apart, it makes not one iota of difference to the believing child of God. We are stormproof. Inflation, recession, illness, or privation, or suffering, or any horrible period of troubled times—none of these things can shake the confidence and faith of the trusting Jesus person.

It used to be that only fundamentalists were preaching the doomsday messages. Today you can hardly pick up a paper or tune in a news program without hearing the trumpet of disaster. Historian Geoffrey Barraclaugh screams out a warning about total collapse in *The Great World Crisis*. *The New York Times* has been documenting scary series about worldwide famine. Magazines and commentaries warn about military intervention in the Middle East. Scientists warn that exhaust from superjets and aerosol sprays may deplete the ozone layer that protects human life from cancer-producing ultraviolet rays. Climatologists speculate the earth may be nearing another ice age. Alvin Toffler, the author of *Future Shock,* predicts our nation is suffering ecospasms that will lead to an apocalypse. Even the movie producers are joining the fright parade, with films like *The Towering Inferno, Earthquake,* and other horrifiers.

Recently, Robert Heilbroner, a famous economist, suggested man's greatest problem now is "how to summon up the will to survive." In his new book, *The End of Affluence,* Paul Ehrlich advises would-be survivors to head for the hills or return to the bomb shelters. Bible scholars warn that society is overripe for a major breakdown.

Rod MacLeish recently coined the term "bleak chic"—suggesting how fashionable it has now become to dwell on depression news. A wave of disaster warnings is sweeping the world.

6. Bad News That Is Really Good News

Now there appears to be a revolt against bad news. People turn off news programs and attempt to shut out all pessimistic reports. The world seems ripe for encouragement and good news. Yet that is exactly what Christians have been trying to say ever since the first warnings were sounded: "The bad news is really good news!" A paradox? No! Those who believe the Bible understood that all these things must come to pass before the end comes. Christians rejoice because all the bad news is a series of signposts clearly marked out on their roadmap to eternity. Each terrifying event more clearly pinpoints our position down the homestretch.

The Bible says when darkness overtakes us, God's light will come bursting in. Listen to it:

> When darkness overtakes him, light will come bursting in. He is kind and merciful—and all goes well for the generous man who conducts his business fairly. Such a man will not be overthrown by evil circumstances. God's constant care of him will make a deep impression on all who see it. He does not fear bad news, nor live in dread of what may happen. For he is settled in his mind that Jehovah will take care of him. That is why he is not afraid, but can calmly face his foes. He gives generously to those in need. His deeds will never be forgotten. He shall have influence and honor.
>
> (Psalms 112:4–9 LB)

God never sleeps and He is always watching. He told us His eye is on the righteous and His ear is open to their cry. Bad news got you down? Worried about slipping or getting hurt? Troubled about the coming violence and unemployment? Then listen to this:

> He will never let me stumble, slip or fall. For he is always watching, never sleeping. Jehovah himself is caring for you! He is your defender. He protects you day and night. He keeps you from all evil, and preserves your life. He keeps his eye upon you as you come and go, and always guards you.
>
> (Psalms 121:3–8 LB)

Christian, you dare not stay up late at night and fret over conditions. Be aware and take all of God's warnings to heart. But after you have done all you can, then sit back, go to sleep, and trust God. God said:

It is senseless for you to work so hard from early morning until late at night, fearing you will starve to death; for God wants his loved ones to get their proper rest.

(Psalms 127:2 LB)

You can be very sure that the evil man will not go unpunished forever. And you can also be very sure that God will rescue the children of the godly. The good man can look forward to happiness, while the wicked can expect only wrath.

(Proverbs 11:21,23 LB)

No real harm befalls the good, but there is constant trouble for the wicked.

(Proverbs 12:21 LB)

The Lord is a strong fortress. The godly run to him and are safe. The rich man thinks of his wealth as an impregnable defense, a high wall of safety. What a dreamer!

(Proverbs 18:10,11 LB)

12

What a Wonderful Day to Be Living in— For Christians, That Is!

I read the papers and watch the news in a day and age that seems to be hopeless. Any average world-watcher sees the handwriting on the wall. Famine stalks the earth like an enraged lion, and millions face starvation. The world economy is so jittery, almost any exploding fear crisis could trigger collapse. Armageddon looms on the horizon. A nation that can't cope with handguns, heroin, or pornography will not be able to cope with hydrogen bombs in the hands of radicals. With the ghosts of depression, unemployment, anarchy, and moral depravity lingering in the shadows, there appears to be very little to be cheerful about!

But, I am a Christian—and that makes all the difference in the world in how I look at the events of today and the dangers of the future. Any genuine Christian will be infected by fear and depression if he feeds only on the bad news coming at him from all directions. It is one thing to stay well informed, but it is dangerous to live on a diet of despair, gloom, and fear. The Christian who lives his life looking for Christ's appearing will gladly receive all warnings, visions, and prophecies that are scripturally sound. *But warnings to "flee from the wrath of God" are for sinners, not Christians. And God will not allow any true shepherd to frighten His flock with false messages designed only to strike fear in their hearts.*

There is a new flood of visions, dreams, predictions, dire warnings, and prophecies. Ministers and mystics alike are now jumping on the apocalyptic bandwagon, and the result is an avalanche of fearmongering and false hope.

There is an easy solution to the problem of discerning which message is right and which is wrong. The only message for overcoming, victorious Christians is that which proclaims deliverance and hope!

Through all true visions, prophecies, or warnings, this message must come through clear and certain: "God has everything under control, and His people have nothing to fear." Those who know where they stand with the Lord can rejoice with every trumpet

sounding. And as the events begin to unfold as prophesied, they look up and rejoice, because they are already
redeemed by faith.

Let me tell you why this is such a wonderful day in
which to be living—for Christians, that is. It is based on
some very simple but too often overlooked facts. Let me
list just a few:

1. God Isn't Dead After All!

His enemies tried to bury Him and proclaimed a new
day of "freedom from the tyranny of God." The educators, philosophers, and liberal theologians were going to
deliver this generation from ignorance, poverty, and immorality. The "green revolution" envisioned by experts
would provide adequate food for the world. Billions
spent in the field of education would foster a generation
of young minds whose think tanks would offer solutions
to problems once thought unsolvable. The promulgation
of liberated sex attitudes and the lifting of all restraints
would produce an era free from moral hangups and
wipe out perversion. With God out of the way, man
thought he could conquer not only the moon but the
universe. And it was a wild, heady ride while it lasted.
Prosperity became intoxicating. The cornucopia of
abundance seemed to have no bottom. Cities spent with
abandon. Promises were piled upon promises. Innova-
tion, expansion, and success were the key words. Men
shook the dust of the moon off their feet. Unions made
ridiculous demands and industry relented—for, after
all, there seemed to be no end to consumer demand.
Silver and gold became the national altar, and materialism became the new god. Ungodly men laughed and by
their actions were saying, "If God is not dead, He is
unimportant—and we are doing quite well without
Him, thank you!"

But God would not play the game. He refused to roll
over and play dead, but instead shook Himself like a

giant awakening from slumber. The earth began to tremble. Deadly arrows of famine came streaking from His presence, ending the green revolution and shattering the predictions of worldwide abundance. Cities began to crumble and decay. The queen city of our nation, proud and arrogant, wallowed in chaotic disarray. Crime spread like cancer. Drug and alcoholic abuse became pandemic. Suddenly there was confusion and bewilderment everywhere. Nations woke up on the brink of bankruptcy. Unemployment exploded like a bomb. Schools became battlegrounds, and the great educators and experts couldn't even isolate the problems, let alone offer solutions. A flood of filth inundated the earth. From Copenhagen to California an outbreak of nudity, rape, perversion, and smut got out of control. Sadly, the new freedom only made more slaves and neurotics.

The Christian must realize what happened and rejoice. God is simply making His statement! He is saying, "The nations of this world are but a drop in the bucket . . . as small dust . . ." (Isaiah 40:15).

I am glad to be alive this day to behold the same display of God's power and glory that Moses and the Israelites witnessed centuries ago! Once again God's glory is seen in awesome demonstrations of power that confuse and bewilder kings, presidents, and the masses everywhere. God is doing exactly what He said He would do. He is pouring out His Spirit upon all flesh. On the believer, as a "baptizing, purifying Spirit" that springs up like a well within. On the ungodly, that Spirit falls as fire and sits upon the heads of the wicked as judgment.

God is walking on the wicked just as the prophet Malachi said He would:

And ye shall tread down the wicked; for they shall be ashes under the soles of your feet in the day that I shall do this, saith the Lord of hosts.

Malachi 4:3 KJV

Look around you, Christian friend, at all the fearful signs and wonders happening. Then be glad you have lived to see the day that shall not pass till all His Word is fulfilled.

2. God Delights in Delivering His People From Hard Times.

As surely as God hates to send judgment on the wicked, He loves to send deliverance to the righteous. Paul understood the true nature of God—severe on the wicked and good to the righteous:

> Behold therefore the goodness and severity of God: on them which fell, severity; but toward thee, goodness, if thou continue in his goodness: otherwise thou also shalt be cut off.
>
> (Romans 11:22 KJV)

If you really understand the nature of God, and if you know His record in the Word for delivering, there is no way at all you can be afraid of the future. Look at the record.

God revealed to Moses the reasons why He sends judgment, plagues, and calamities upon a society: "I will multiply my signs and wonders upon Egypt . . . that I may lay my hand upon Egypt . . . and deliver my people . . . by great judgments . . ." (Exodus 7:3, 4).

For the same reasons, God is judging our world right now. He must get His hands on the wicked and at the same time deliver His children. *Judgment is a process of deliverance as well as retribution!*

Talk about hard times, calamities, and judgment! Invasions of frogs, lice, disease, locusts, and hail! The stench of death. Destruction of all cattle, all trees, and everything green.

Listen to this:
- ". . . and frogs came up and covered the land."
- ". . . and the houses of the Egyptians swarmed with flies."
- ". . . and all the cattle of Egypt died."
- ". . . and boils broke forth upon man and beast."
- ". . . and the Lord sent thunder and hail, and the fire ran along the ground."
- ". . . and locusts covered the face of the land, and the land was darkened."
- ". . . and thick darkness covered all of Egypt three days."
- ". . . and the Lord smote all the firstborn of Egypt."

Meanwhile, at the Israelite camp in Goshen, things were different. Does God take delight in saving His people in the day of wrath? You must believe it! "And I will put a division between my people and thy people . . . and I will sever in that day the land of Goshen . . ." (Exodus 8:23,22 KJV).

While judgment was falling on the wicked, God was busy showing His power to deliver the righteous.

- ". . . the land of Egypt was corrupted by flies . . . *but no flies shall swarm in Goshen, that thou mayest know that I am the Lord in the midst of the earth.*"
- ". . . and the Lord severed between the cattle of Israel and the cattle of Egypt . . . and all the cattle of Egypt died; *but of the cattle of Israel died not one.*"
- ". . . and hail smote throughout all the land of Egypt, all that was in the field, both man and beast; *only in the land of Goshen, where the children of Israel were, was there no hail.*"
- ". . . and there was a thick darkness in all the

land of Egypt three days . . . *but the children of Israel had light in their dwellings.*"

● ". . . and there shall be a great cry throughout all the land of Egypt . . . and all the firstborn shall die . . . *but against any of the children of Israel shall not a dog move his tongue . . . that ye may know that the Lord doth put a difference between the Egyptians and Israelites.*"

God still puts a difference between the wicked and the righteous.

For God hath not appointed us to wrath, but to obtain salvation by our Lord Jesus Christ.

(1 Thessalonians 5:9 KJV)

Much more then, being justified by his blood, *we shall be saved from wrath through him.*

(Romans 5:9 KJV)

. . . even Jesus, *which delivered us from the wrath to come.*

(1 Thessalonians 1:10 KJV)

The prophet Malachi foresaw our day and predicted God would stay true to His nature—swift judgment on the wicked of the last generation and deliverance for the godly.

But who may abide the day of his coming? and who shall stand when he appeareth? . . . And I will come near to you to judgment; and I will be a swift witness against the sorcerers, and against the adulterers, false swearers, oppressors, and those who fear me not . . . Ye are cursed with a curse; for ye have robbed me, even this whole nation.

(Malachi 3:2,5,9)

And while God is sending judgment on drug abusers, wife cheaters, liars, and agnostics, look at what He is doing for those who prove Him:

Prove me now . . . saith the Lord of hosts, if I will not open you the windows of heaven, and pour you out a blessing, that there shall not be room enough to receive it. And I will rebuke the devourer for your sakes, and he shall not destroy the fruits of your ground; neither shall your vine cast her fruit before the time in the field, saith the Lord of hosts.
(Malachi 3:10,11 KJV)

Malachi warned conditions would become "oven hot" for the wicked: "For, behold, the day cometh, that shall burn as an oven; and all the proud, yea, and all that do wickedly, shall burn as stubble . . ." (Malachi 4:1).

And while the wicked are left without root or fruit, God has promised something very miraculous for the righteous: "But unto you that fear my name shall the Sun of righteousness arise with healing in his wings; and ye shall go forth, and grow up . . ." (Malachi 4:2 KJV).

Why is this such a glorious day in which to be living? Because the beginning of sorrows for the wicked is the beginning of final deliverance for the righteous. It is the world's hour of tribulation and wrath—but an hour of miracles and promises for the godly. It is a day wherein Christians are going to realize the great difference faith makes. Today we know what Paul meant when he said, "God has provided some better things for us . . ." (Hebrews 4:10).

3. We Don't Belong Here Anyhow!

Everything is going to burn, and who wants to be left holding ashes? "Seeing then that all these things shall be dissolved, what manner of persons ought ye to be in all holy conversation and godliness?" (2 Peter 3:11 KJV).

Did you ever stop to think how frail and insecure all worldly things are?

- ". . . buildings that decay, leaving not a single stone upon another."
- ". . . bags with holes in them . . . wells without water . . . clouds without rain."
- ". . . things that burn . . . elements that melt . . . materials that dissolve."
- ". . . lust that kills . . . pleasures that end up in pain . . . joys that turn into sorrows."
- ". . . storehouses where goods rust and thieves break in and steal."
- ". . . big loaded barns left for others to enjoy . . . houses, lands, fields left to others."
- ". . . wealth, honor and power—yet God giveth him no power to eat thereof, but a stranger eateth it."
- ". . . labor for food, yet the appetite unfulfilled."
- ". . . riches kept for the owner's hurt . . . riches that perish by evil travail."
- ". . . wine that mocks . . . children who are disobedient . . . wives that betray."

We think of Sodom and remember fire and brimstone. God said, "Remember Lot's wife!" She was so attached to her little world, she couldn't give it up even after it all melted with fervent heat. When judgment fires fall again over this old earth, many will be dragged into eternity, kicking and screaming—not over their lost souls but their lost things!

Paul spoke of "a certain fearful looking for of judgment and fiery indignation, which shall devour the adversaries"—but as "the day" approached, Christians "took joyfully the spoiling of their goods, knowing in themselves that they had in heaven a better and enduring substance" (Hebrews 10:27,34).

The coming economic upheavals will spoil a lot of people's goods. Those who are living only for today will be devastated with fears their good life will be spoiled

147

for them. But God's people look for a new Heaven and a new earth. We are moving, and the Mover is already at our door. And, we must travel light. We gladly will over to the enemy all our earthly goods—donated as kindling for the coming fire.

Right in the middle of all the warnings of spoiled goods, reproaches, and afflictions, we read: *"Now,* the just shall live by faith . . ."* (Hebrews 10:38).

Now is the time to live a new lifestyle—completely by faith. And we have missed entirely the meaning of faith described in Hebrews:

> Now faith is the substance of things hoped for,
> the evidence of things not seen.
>
> (Hebrews 11:1 KJV)

God is trying to tell us about a whole new concept of things with spiritual substance. We are told not to give any thought to things we eat or drink or wear. But the things faith produces are not made of physical, material substance. These things are given to God's children simply because He knows they are needed—and He supplies all their needs as a matter of fact and promise. Oh, but there is hope for things beyond this fleeting life. Things like appearing before Him in Zion. Walking right into His courts with praise and thanksgiving, leaping and praising God in a new and glorified body. Living under your own vine and fig tree, without war or disease, famine or fear. Living through a thousand years a day. Touching the very substance of everything I hoped for but could not see.

Why are these such good days to be living in—for Christians, that is? Because it is the last day! And there has to be a last day here before there can be a first day there!

The next time you begin to fret and worry about our crumbling society, just keep reminding yourself, "I don't belong here anymore, anyhow!"

148

The alarm has sounded—listen and fear!
For I, the Lord, am sending disaster into your
land. But always, first of all, I warn you
through my prophets. This I now have done.

Amos 3:6,7 LB

13

You Can Know You Are Ready!

The Bible says: "Ye shall know the truth, and the truth shall set you free" (John 8:32). This makes it very clear that you will not really be free until you understand what the truth of salvation is. So few people know what it means to be "saved." Let's talk sense about it!

It is not enough to "get bugged" by a sermon, to shed a few tears, to "decide" for Christ, to say a nice little prayer in private, to think up some good thoughts of faith and hope when alone, to turn over a new leaf to ease the conscience. I am going to show you—plain and simple—how you must cooperate with God in order to *know* you are saved, so that Satan cannot come to you *after* your conversion to snatch away your experience.

1. First of all, let's talk about what you really are without Christ:

Admit it! You are a sinner—a real rebel! You are a rebel against God's rulership in your life, and you live only to suit yourself, regardless of how it affects God or other people. Self is "king of the hill" in your heart! You go your own way. According to the Bible, sinners are stubborn, disobedient, spoiled, distorted in moral values, deceitful, wrong, and rebellious against authority. Sin makes one an enemy to God.

God promised to save you from sin, but first you must really understand what sin is. Sin is a refusal to live intelligently or to conform our lives to the truth of God's Word. It is not just a *weakness* but a state of rebellion. You do not sin because you don't understand—but because you refuse to recognize your very clear obligations to God and man. Now God has honestly promised you mercy, pardon, peace, and happiness—but only on *His* terms.

Without Christ you have a crippled conscience. The apostle Paul described it as "a mind and conscience that is defiled" (Titus 1:15). The conscience is an endowed part of your personality, given for the purpose of evaluating your conduct and behavior to your own heart. God designed it to "smile" when your conduct is right and to "frown" when it is wrong. God intended this faculty to be an instrument of blessing, to bring tranquility and inner composure. But sin in your life has tampered with that tender conscience and left it in a state of gloom and fear. The marvelous effect of salvation is the mysterious healing of the conscience.

Yes—without Christ, you are a rebel, and you don't deserve pity: you have a will and can be held accountable for your own sin. There is no such thing as a "helpless sinner." You are not responsible for the sin of Adam and Eve; you are responsible for your own. The Gospel is bad news to those who live for self and good news only to those who surrender intelligently.

2. Now let's talk about how the wheels of your salvation start in motion!

The disciples asked the Lord, "Who then can be saved?" Jesus answered, "With men it is impossible, but not with God: for with God all things are possible" (Mark 10:26–27 KJV). Salvation is a cooperative effort. God initiates the action and man reacts. God cannot do your part, and you cannot do God's part. No man is convicted and converted accidentally. *Never!* There are powerful unseen forces at work, striving with your entire being. God uses these forces to induce us to repent. First of all, the Holy Spirit fights for your soul, striving and restraining, showing you how exceedingly sinful sin actually is. The Word of God is a force pulling on your heart, showing you the "goodness of God that leads to repentance" (Romans 2:4).

When the message from God's Word gets through to you, it hits you hard—like a hammer breaking a heart of stone. It brings powerful Holy Ghost conviction upon you and exposes all hidden sin in your life. God also uses friends to lead you to Christ. A true friend will talk to you about the wrath of God, the terror of hell, the joy of Heaven, and the tender compassion of a loving Savior. God uses the Holy Spirit, the Holy Word, to change your good intentions into an act of true repentance.

Do you think it is an accident that this message is

151

delivered to you? Do you think God is not concerned about you—how you live and how you think? Get that out of your mind. All the forces of Heaven are turned on you; you are under the influence of the "outpouring of the Holy Ghost," and you must face an hour of truth! When the Holy Ghost pulls, it's time for you to push—into the Kingdom!

3. Salvation doesn't really count until you truly repent!

"Joy shall be in heaven over one sinner that repenteth . . ." (Luke 15:7 KJV). Repentance can never be anything but your very own act. God will use forces to draw us but will never coerce our wills. Only you can turn the rudder of the ship of life into waters of obedience. Neither God nor man can repent for us. Listen! Your salvation hinges on one thing—Will you *turn from sin,* or will you not? Too many people have been self-deceived—and have gone to their doom thinking they were on their way to Heaven—because they failed to understand what it means to repent!

Salvation without true repentance is absolutely impossible, and anyone who thinks it is possible is "seeking refuge in lies" (Isaiah 28:17).

Repentance begins with a revelation and an admission of personal guilt. You cannot blame parents or environment or use any pathetic excuses of psychiatrists. You must feel the guilt—admit you are in darkness and that you are condemned and unable to save yourself. Have you honestly and clearly admitted, "I am a guilty sinner. I am lost. I have grieved God. I have lived only for myself. I am sorry"? This you *must* do!

Repentance means to change one's mind. It is a climactic revolution of the mind concerning God, self, sin, and the will. God is waiting to see how honest your repentance will be. When you pray, "Lord, I repent," you are actually promising: "Lord, I've changed my mind about everything. I see what sin did to me. I am tired of selfish living, and I surrender my will to You. Crush my own ambitions, and put within me a new heart."

Repentance is a complete turn away from being a rebel, from foolish and ungodly friends, from conformity with the world, from secret sins and habits of the flesh, from filthy books, from dirty stories and unclean jokes, from unintelligent living and planning, from wasting time, from everything and everybody that would hinder you from being a 100-percent follower of Christ.

So you see, friend, "I repent" is more than two little words prayed when under the influence of an emotional experience. It is a revolution, a way of life, a surrender, a declaration of new allegiance, a submission, a pledge to denounce the world once and for all. Christ must become your commander-in-chief, or you are still an unrepentant rebel. Stop being a little god to yourself; surrender your sword of bitterness; raise your flag of surrender; and put your life under new management.

Once you repent, "you are not your own; you are bought with a price" (1 Corinthians 6:19,20). You cannot have Christ and ungodly friends too. Choose Christ or the crowd—right now! You will never be able to stay "up tight" with God until you give up everything for the "knowledge of salvation."

4. Faith is the power that initiates and continues your conversion!

God may be willing to forgive and restore you, and you may be ever so willing to forsake sin and follow Christ—yet no salvation can take place without a very important step being taken to walk in the path of holiness. That great step is *faith!* A great number of passages in the Bible make it very plain that the benefits of salvation become effective only by faith.

Faith is not a mere intellectual state of belief but a complete committal of the will and a full trust and confidence that our sins are forever forgiven by the sacrificial sufferings of Christ on the cross.

Wherever Jesus preached repentance, He preached faith as a follow-up. So did all of His disciples. Their message was: ". . . repentance toward God and faith toward our Lord Jesus Christ" (Acts 20:21 KJV).

Jesus said: "Repent ye, and believe the gospel" (Mark 1:15 KJV). "He that believeth on me hath everlasting life. I am that bread of life" (John 6:47,48 KJV.)

The faith I am talking about requires much deep thinking. Your mind can't drift in neutral with hopes based on nothing more than happy feelings or "joy pop" religion. Your faith will shift into gear only as you feed on the Word of God and understand what it promises.

You know good and well that faith is not just a feeling or impulse. Some "converts" revert to the old life of fear and doubt, then critically cry, "I didn't get anything; I don't understand; I don't feel a thing"—because they do not possess faith. They do not want to strain their minds, so they decide their salvation didn't take. You must prop up your faith with Bible truth and say once and for all, "God said it! I believe it! That settles it!"

God's Word says, "Repent, believe, and have everlasting life." Stake your life on it! It's true; believe every word of it; your salvation depends on it!

There is one Scripture in the Bible that should give you all the faith you need to continue in your salvation. Memorize it:

Being confident of this very thing, that he which hath begun a good work in you will perform it until the day of Jesus Christ.

(Philippians 1:6 KJV)

5. Now, let's talk sense about how Christians should act!

First of all, you have to purpose in your heart to "stick to the Lord" (Acts 11:23). Salvation is not a state of fear but of happy persuasion that "Christ is all in all" (Colossians 3:11). Obey the command of the Lord: "Keep yourselves in the love of God, looking for the mercy of our Lord Jesus Christ unto eternal life" (Jude 21 KJV).

You must continue in the state of repentance and faith. Pray for boldness to tell others what Christ can do. Expect to be persecuted and rejected by those who are still in darkness. Expect to find some hyprocrites even in the best churches. Don't set your eyes on people, because humans fail—only God doesn't. Allow the Holy Spirit to deal honestly with you about smoking, drinking, sex attitudes, and dress. Don't be a phony. Don't hide behind a false front; be honest!

Don't worry about getting depressed or blue—even Paul the Apostle had that problem. When you are blue, worried, or perplexed, stay true by staying on your knees in your bedroom until the load is lifted. Read your Bible every single day. Pray at least fifteen minutes each day. Don't leave the house or go to bed at night without talking to Jesus.

If your church is dead and you begin to grow cold spiritually, pray for your minister. Go to him, and tell him you want to see more of the dynamics of the Holy Spirit in the church and in your life. Start a prayer group with some of your friends. If that doesn't work, find a friend who is "on fire" for God and go with him or her to church.

Seek to be filled with the Spirit. Present your body to the Lord to be used in full-time Christian service. If you are convinced God wants you to serve Him in secular work, make all your plans in partnership with the Lord. Acknowledge Him for all directions.

Once you take your stand for Christ, don't expect to be converted over and over again. Trust your conversion as final as long as you walk with Christ.

14

A LETTER TO THE PRESIDENT OF
THE UNITED STATES

Dear Sir:

The Bible has much to say to our president and America at this particular time. From its prophecies, we must recognize that this nation is at a pivotal point. Two ways lie before us: one of righteousness with God or one of rejection because of pride. The Bible says, "Righteousness exalteth a nation, but sin is a reproach to any nation."

You, as president, have a choice to show a spiritually hungry world what God can do for a nation whose leader is not ashamed to proclaim faith in Him.

God wants to unite Himself with the leaders of this nation—*Now*—to bring about a new capacity for humility and love. Repentance gives a nation the right to God's resources, and humility gives access to true prosperity and peace. National unbelief must now give way to honesty with God.

Mr. President, we believe your claim to be a Christian. We know, therefore, there is one thing you can never be, and that is silent about it. To know Christ is to inevitably proclaim His love and power in every aspect of life. Christ cannot be subjugated by party politics. He must not be drowned out by Potomac fever. He can never take second place to policy or expediency. You can separate politics from religion but not from Christ!

Others of us who claim to be born-again believe God is giving America her final call to repentance and humility. We believe the president must say in his inaugural address what God wants to hear. He must not be snubbed or given just a formal acknowledgement. God is waiting for your direct public and shameless appeal for His help and guidance.

We pray for you, Mr. President! You deserve time to put into practice what you really believe. But, time is running out. A porno plague must be stopped. Violence must be curbed. The moral landslide must end. Righteousness, truth, and the exaltation of God must be experienced by all.

God's final trumpets are sounding, and this nation and its leaders had better catch step with its high mission. We can no longer keep hiding from a voice that keeps sounding in our ears.

There is a surplus of guilt in the American soul. It is more than just a growing sense that we have offended against the welfare of the human race. It is a growing sense that there is something called sin in the world and that God must see it either forsaken or judged. And, the majority of people of this nation do want God involved in all our affairs. They know we can no longer be left to our own devices on the wrinkled, worn-out skin of this pigmy planet!

In this crisis time, the American people must learn the lessons of history. History repeats itself, and God said what happened to past societies can happen to this society. They decayed and crumbled because of corruption.

In six thousand years, we have fashioned twenty odd civilizations and destroyed every one. Today we are nearer than we ever were before to the possibility of self-extinction.

We have seen what happened to nations who just didn't seem to think God was necessary anymore. With God, gone, they got Communism, Fascism, and Nazism. When God is no longer the hitching post for a nation's morality, a dreadful and abysmal sense of futility follows. The only goal then becomes comfort and the protection of national pride. When a people lose their consciousness of God, they lose their aim in life, and then it is no trick at all to fool mankind into any kind of surrender you plan for him.

The pressure of God on our national soul has never been greater than it is right now. To betray it now would be to wear thin the patience of God with our generation. We can no longer afford to idle away our time while our civilization staggers down another God-forsaken road to ruin. It's time to get down to rock bottom, because the problem of freedom has now become religious.

We have whittled down God almost to a vanishing point. Nothing more than a dream of sleepy preachers. We have tried to make Him obsolete. We have tried to maneuver and manipulate Him as though He were some kind of vest-pocket edition of our own fantasies. No wonder our nation is forever trying to interpret its own confusion. Really, there isn't nearly the confusion around as some would have you think; there is plenty of downright avoidance—of God. Unless we prefer to be confused, there is a way out! That way out is through humility and repentance, from the White House down through the county courthouses.

This nation has many who would "sneer" God out of the minds of our young. Large sections of our population now engage in cheap ridicule of puritanism. The word itself arouses contempt. The sophisticated intellectuals regard the founding Puritan fathers as comic figures. In all the media, wit and mockery are used to cleverly and sarcastically put down the moral codes of the past. It is a design to create a flippant atmosphere in which Christian morals come across "awfully funny." Television especially wallows in ghastly comedy aimed at giggling away standards once considered honorable. How can God long spare a nation that makes science so sure and God so "creepy"? Agnostics want it believed that Christian ethics is a morality for slaves. A spiritual awakening can turn this tide, almost overnight. You have the power to help turn the tide.

We realize the president can't do it all. But, we believe America is in a mood to respond to a national call to renewed faith and trust in God. Bible history clearly reveals that the fate of nations depended upon the spiritual bend of their leaders. When spiritual leaders used their power to execute righteousness before God and the nation, prosperity and peace always followed. When the leaders turned away from God and compromised, trouble erupted on all fronts. Jewish history is filled with such examples.

1. King Jehoshaphat used the power of his office to clean up the courts and bring judges back to true values—

> He said to the judges, Take heed what you do; for you judge not for man, but for the Lord . . . wherefore now let the fear of the Lord be upon you: for God will not put up with iniquity, nor favoring certain people, nor the taking of bribes. . . .
> (II Chronicles 19:6–7 KJV, Paraphrased.)

This godly leader "set himself to seek the Lord." He encouraged the nation to "ask help of the Lord" in their hour of crisis. He proclaimed a national time of fasting and prayer. At his bidding, all the nation "stood before the Lord." The leader and all the citizens cried out, "In God's hand is all the power and might, and none will be able to withstand Him."

> So the realm of Jehoshaphat was quiet; for his God gave him rest round about . . .

> He waxed great exceedingly . . . he built cities . . . he had much business . . . people had valor . . . even Arabians brought gifts . . . and the fear of God fell upon all the kingdoms round about"
> (II Chronicles 17:10–19 KJV, Paraphrased.)

2. The Bible speaks of another time and society that was vexed with turbulence. The whole world was sick.

And in those times there was no peace to him that went out, nor to him that came in, but great vexations were upon the inhabitants of the countries . . . and nation was destroyed of nation, and city of city: for God did vex them with all adversity

(II Chronicles 15:5,6 KJV.)

God, in His mercy, destined a great leader to bring people together. His name was Asa, a leader the Bible says "who did that which was right in the eyes of the Lord his God."

This chosen man was confronted by the prophet Azariah with this warning,

The Lord is with you, while you are with him; and if you seek him, he will be found of you; but if you forsake him, he will forsake you

(II Chronicles 15:2 LB, Paraphrased.)

King Asa, in a troubled and turbulent hour, led all of Israel back to the God of their fathers. The Bible says, "He commanded them to seek the Lord of their fathers, and to obey the law and the commandments . . ." The people gladly responded. The result? They rebuilt cities. They prospered beyond all that could be imagined. The country had peace. They grew powerful and strong. All because "We sought the Lord our God, and He has given us rest on every side. So they built and prospered"

(II Chronicles 14:7 LB, Paraphrased.)

3. King Jehoram came into power during a time of great prosperity and peace in Israel. But "he did that which was evil in the eyes of the Lord." He led his people into compromise, dishonesty, and bribery. Suddenly, a nation that enjoyed peace and prosperity was threatened with war by the Philistines and Arabians. Enemies "carried away all their substance." And this man died with an incurable disease, for "God smote him" after only eight years in office. And he was buried with no public mourning, having become very unpopular.

(II Chronicles 21 LB, Paraphrased.)

4. King Abijah was a leader who stood before his nation and cried unashamedly from a mountaintop, "As for us, the Lord is our God, and we have not forsaken Him . . ."

Facing fantastic odds, God miraculously intervened, and Judah was victorious against an army that outnumbered it two to one. History records this insight: And the children of Judah prevailed, because they relied upon the Lord God of their fathers . . .

(II Chronicles 13:1–12 LB, Paraphrased.)

5. King Jehu was a leader who came to power in times similar to these. His inauguration to office filled many with dismay, while exciting others with the highest of hopes. The worshippers of God had been mourning the degeneracy of the times and sighed and prayed for a spiritual renewal.

It seemed their prayers were answered, and they thought they recognized in this man just brought to office one who would use his great zeal and ambition to save the nation from the whirlpool of ruin into which it was rapidly sinking.

He came to power out of nowhere. His language was one of pious politics. He spoke sincerely and boldly of reform. He was one of those decisive, ambitious, calculating, passionate men whom God, from time to time, raises up to change the fate of nations and to fulfill His will.

Supposing him to have been, by conviction, a true follower of the Lord, believers gave him their favor. He was such a man of action, organization, and contemplation, the entire nation was filled with new hope. He had a sense of destiny about him.

The nation was reeling from the impact of a wicked, fallen government. Its former leader had fallen as a result of a moral landslide.

Flagrant immorality had caused the government to collapse, and its leader had become a social leper who was living as an outcast in a secluded house, a man forgotten and out of mind.

Corruption and bribery in high places had brought about a savage hunger for truth and righteousness. The nation had experienced the trauma of a high level massacre, and a leadership vacuum had developed.

Into this vacuum came a new face! One of the most apparently honest the nation had ever seen came to power. No one questioned his sincerity. He appeared to have a firm faith, combined with a strict and earnest life, compelling respect even from his enemies.

This man was not afraid to mix religion with politics; he seemed to be as much interested in righteousness as revenue; he believed God's grace was needed in government; he claimed to be born again with a holy zeal; he called for the protection of the Jewish faith; his thirst for power seemed directed toward spiritual renewal; he stated that the national government was obligated to protect the spiritual freedom of its people; and he seemed like such a plain man identifying with plain folk.

But, King Jehu failed in his mission. The bottom line proved to be pride and self-achievement. His zeal for God cooled when it required him to take a direction contrary to his own will. Jehu was not truly reformed or committed, and consequently his spiritual revolution failed.

This highly-praised leader refused to deal with the great sins of his nation, because he was afraid to confront those who gave him his authority. He feared losing his popularity if he called for a complete return to righteousness. He had used religion to ride to power, but now it was exposed as a shallow hypocrisy.

The man who was called by God to be "an instrument of righteousness" rejected his destiny and succumbed to the wicked counsel of evil advisors. The Bible says, "Jehu took no heed to walk in the law of the Lord God . . . with all his heart." His religion gave way to his politics. He became more concerned about getting a firm grip on power than allowing God to get a firm grip on him.

Believers in Israel realized they had been deceived. The national spirit was broken, its prestige dimmed, and helpless bewilderment became widespread. A nation that had so desperately bound together in hope for a new direction began to fall under divine judgment. In pursuit of establishing his own royal dynasty, King Jehu gave in to the seductive power of unbelief. Unwilling to do what God told him to do, he paralyzed the spiritual mood of the nation. His reign ended in the worse kind of apostasy and disaster. It ended in horrible calamity and crime. The nation was weakened, and enemies extracted its wealth.

This great leader compromised so blatantly, his government became an insult to God. And a man who could have forever lifted a curse from a doomed nation ended up just another politician, obsessed by a lust for power.

Mr. President, may you and all our people heed these Biblical words:

Now all these things happened unto them for ensamples: and they were written for our admonition, upon whom the ends of the world are come

(I Corinthians 10:11 KJV.)

God raised you up for such an hour as this. Never be ashamed of Jesus Christ. Tell the world that He is the real Peacemaker. Follow the example of the righteous leaders of Israel.

Bow before God daily, stretch forth your hands to Heaven, and pray, imploring His mercy on this nation. Millions throughout the land are willing to lay on the counter of human life the price of personal responsibility. Believers throughout the world will be holding you up in prayer.

There are a growing number of American Christians who now sense a divine foreboding. They hear the sound of a trumpet, a last call to repentance. God's subterranean thunder is already roaring forth a warning. Earthquakes, droughts, and financial crises were called, in

Bible times, "instruments of judgment." This nation can no longer flirt with such ominous retribution. Judgment will result from the wrong we have done to the love God is trying to show us.

What does it take to save a society from judgment? The answer is found at Nineveh. The repentance of that society as a result of Jonah's warning is one of the great events in history. It will take the very same intense repentance and reform to save America. All the praying and talking in the world will not save our nation, unless it produces "Nineveh-like" repentance.

1. They believed the warnings of coming judgment! A fast was proclaimed, and the entire society was "awed" by the fear of God. It started a revolution of repentance. The masses forsook their pursuit of pleasure. Violence and sensuality were dealt a stunning blow, and crime was punished severely—all by decree from the government. The proud wept in sorrow, and phony forms of religion were swept away by a complete turning to God. They said,

> Who can tell if God will turn and repent, and turn away from his fierce anger, that we perish not?

> (Jonah 3:9 KJV.)

2. All of society was affected! It became a time of national soul-searching. The rich and poor, government and society leaders, the good and the bad—all humbled themselves in true sorrow for sin. It was not just a "revival of fear" or a spiritual awakening of a segment. No! It was a top to bottom, through and through, social and spiritual turnaround. Business adjusted its values. The entire population was in agony over sin and rebellion against God. The leaders wept. Days and weeks of prayer and repentance were called for by the official government. Lawmakers turned to God and cried out, "We are sorry. Save us from ourselves."

Jesus warned,

> The men of Nineveh shall rise up in the judgment with this generation, and shall condemn it: for they repented at the preaching of Jonah; and, behold, a greater than Jonah is here.

> (Matthew 12:41 KJV.)

Mr. President, the Bible clearly states what we all must do if your vision for the future of America is to be fulfilled. God's love is endless, and His commandments are not grievous. All He demands is that we love and seek Him with all our hearts, souls, minds, and bodies. That we never become lukewarm in that love. That we love our neighbors as ourselves. That we exalt righteousness and condemn immorality. That spiritual wickedness in high places be fought against. That Christ never be denied before mankind. That He be acknowledged in all our ways. That we confess and forsake our sins.

Not one single American can sit as your judge. God alone is your judge. But, to whom much is given, much is expected. You represent this nation's last hope for a government truly "under God." You must commandeer all our resources to inject God into politics and all our national affairs.

Our government is not absolute in itself; it derives its power from God and exists only as long as God permits it to. Governments rule, not by the consent of men, but by the will of God.

Please sir, use your God-ordained powers to help bring us back to the faith of our fathers.

Yours truly,
CONCERNED CHRISTIANS FOR SPIRITUAL RENEWAL
DAVID WILKERSON, CHAIRMAN